Teaching Handbook Graphic Texts Years 4–6 (P5–7)

Lindsay Pickton and Christine Chen

OXFORD
UNIVERSITY PRESS

Project X *Origins graphic texts* team

Series Editor: Dave Gibbons
Series Consultants: Lindsay Pickton, Christine Chen and Mel Gibson
Guided Reading Notes author team: Lindsay Pickton, Christine Chen and James Clements
Character illustrator: Jonatronix Ltd

The publisher wishes to thank the following schools for their valuable contribution to the trialling and development of **Project X *Origins graphic texts***:

Brinscall St. John's C.E. Methodist Primary School, Chorley; Cairnshill Primary School, Belfast; Christ Church C.E. Junior School, Kent; Dial Park Primary School, Stockport; Good Shepherd Catholic Primary School, London; Ilminster Avenue E-ACT Academy, Bristol; Millennium Primary School, London; Orchard Meadow Primary School, Oxford; Rushmere Hall Primary School, Ipswich; St. Helen's C.E. Primary School, St. Albans; Torridon Junior School, London

OXFORD
UNIVERSITY PRESS

Great Clarendon Street, Oxford, OX2 6DP,
United Kingdom

Oxford University Press is a department of the University of Oxford.
It furthers the University's objective of excellence in research, scholarship,
and education by publishing worldwide. Oxford is a registered trade mark of
Oxford University Press in the UK and in certain other countries

© Oxford University Press 2016

This Edition published in 2016

The moral rights of the author have been asserted

All rights reserved. No part of this publication may be reproduced, stored in
a retrieval system, or transmitted, in any form or by any means, without the
prior permission in writing of Oxford University Press, or as expressly permitted
by law, by licence or under terms agreed with the appropriate reprographics
rights organization. Enquiries concerning reproduction outside the scope of the
above should be sent to the Rights Department, Oxford University Press,
at the address above.

You must not circulate this work in any other form
and you must impose this same condition on any acquirer

ISBN: 978-0-19-836789-5

3 5 7 9 10 8 6 4 2

Paper used in the production of this book is a natural, recyclable product
made from wood grown in sustainable forests. The manufacturing process
conforms to the environmental regulations of the country of origin.

Printed in Great Britain by Ashford Colour Press

Acknowledgements

All photography © OUP except: p78 wong sze yuen/Shutterstock; p81 PeopleImages/iStock

Illustrations by: p 14, p105 Paul Davidson; p15 Alberto Pagliaro; p16 Emily Kimbell; p19 Daniel Duncan; p20 Xavier Bonet; p21, p104 Christian Papazoglakis; p33 Ruben Megido; p37, p100 Jade Sarson; p98 Tom Humberstone; p101 Zosia Dzierżawska; p102 Santy Gutiérrez

PCM illustrations by Thomson Digital

Project X concept by Rod Theodorou and Emma Lynch

Oxford OWL

For school
Discover eBooks, inspirational resources, advice and support

For home
Helping your child's learning with free eBooks, essential tips and fun activities

www.oxfordowl.co.uk

Contents

Welcome to Project X 4

Project X *Origins* 5

Project X *Origins graphic texts* 6

- The importance of graphic texts 14
- Graphic texts and the National Curriculum 16
- Using graphic texts for guided reading 17
- Progression and comprehension in graphic texts 20

How Project X *Origins* can support building an outstanding reading school 24

1. Supporting staff: getting the most out of guided reading 25
- Organizing groups and differentiating learning 25
- The role of the teacher 26
- The importance of talk 27
- Learning from each other 28
- Balancing the needs of the whole class 30

2. Teaching the reading curriculum 32
- Addressing the core reading and spoken language skills 34
- Guided reading progression 37
- The National Curriculum in England 38
    - Years 3 and 4 programme of study 40
    - Years 5 and 6 programme of study 42
    - Spelling, vocabulary, punctuation and grammar coverage 46
- Links to the Scottish Curriculum for Excellence 50
- Links to the Programme of Study for English in Wales 56
- Links to the Northern Ireland Primary Curriculum 64
- Cross-curricular opportunities 70

3. Engaging parents and carers 78

4. Developing the reading environment 81

5. Targeting resources: Oxford Assessment and Levelling 83
- Oxford Reading Criterion Scale: Assessment Standards 5–7 86
- Links to the Oxford Reading Criterion Scale 92
- Oxford Levelling 98

6. Celebrating reading 106
- Photocopiable masters 109

Welcome to Project X

Project X is an innovative reading and writing programme that is rapidly becoming one of the most popular resources in primary schools across the UK. Drawing on research evidence, classroom practice and a real understanding of what makes modern children tick, it has everything you need to make learning both effective and fun.

Engaging group reading with a phonics focus

Reception/P1–Year 1/P2 Fiction and non-fiction books

Effective guided reading starts here!

Reception/P1–Year 6/P7 Fiction and non-fiction books

Taking you on an incredible independent reading journey!

Reception/P1–Year 6/P7

A breakthrough for SEN and struggling readers

Provides rapid catch-up for children from Year 2/P3 onwards

Big Writing Adventures is an award-winning writing programme for Years R–6/Primary 1–7. Oxford University Press has created a series of highly engaging 'writing missions' based on Ros Wilson's powerful **Big Writing** methodology.

Try a free mission at: www.oxfordprimary.co.uk.

Project X *Origins*

Project X *Origins* is a guided reading programme for the whole school. Designed to hook young children into reading in Reception/Primary 1, support them in their early reading development, and turn them into fluent, independent and enthusiastic readers by the time they reach Year 6/P7, **Project X *Origins*** helps you meet the needs of children at every stage of their reading development.

Motivation is crucial to reading success and for this reason, the teaching and learning approaches underpinning **Project X *Origins*** emphasize the importance of comprehension and engagement in learning to read.

What makes Project X *Origins* different?

- **Teaching support:** Project X *Origins* offers comprehensive teaching support, including guidance on comprehension, vocabulary, fluency, spelling, grammar, punctuation and writing to ensure every guided reading session has maximum impact.

- **UK curricula:** Project X *Origins* is fully correlated to all UK curricula, including the new English curriculum and the Programme of Study for English in Wales. In addition, cross-curricular opportunities are provided for every book.

- **Assessment:** formative and summative assessment is supported using the Oxford Reading Criterion Scale to ensure teachers can track and monitor each child's progress and choose exactly the right book to meet each groups' needs.

- **Reading for pleasure:** the learning approaches that underpin **Project X *Origins*** emphasize the importance of comprehension and engagement in learning to read, motivating children and encouraging a habit of reading for pleasure.

- **Reading variety:** Project X *Origins* includes a wide range of books – including graphic texts – to engage every child and ensure they encounter a wide range of genres, broaden their experience, and develop their own reading tastes and enjoyment of reading whole books.

- **Fine levelling:** every **Project X *Origins*** book has been carefully levelled to ensure children encounter the right level of challenge at every stage.

Project X *Origins graphic texts*

At a glance

›› The reading books

The **Project X *Origins graphic texts*** series offers 28 exciting graphic books for children in Years 4–6/P5–7 (Oxford Levels 14–20). The four books at each Oxford Level include one character fiction (featuring the popular **Project X** characters: Max, Cat, Ant and Tiger), one classic fiction, one poetry collection and one non-fiction. For more of a detailed breakdown of the books see page 9.

Books at Oxford Level 18 (Dark Red Book Band)

›› The Guided Reading Notes

Comprehensive Guided Reading Notes are provided for every book, organized into one set of notes for every Oxford Level. The notes include: step-by-step session guidance covering comprehension, vocabulary, spelling, grammar, punctuation and writing; correlation to all UK curricula; and in-built assessment points.

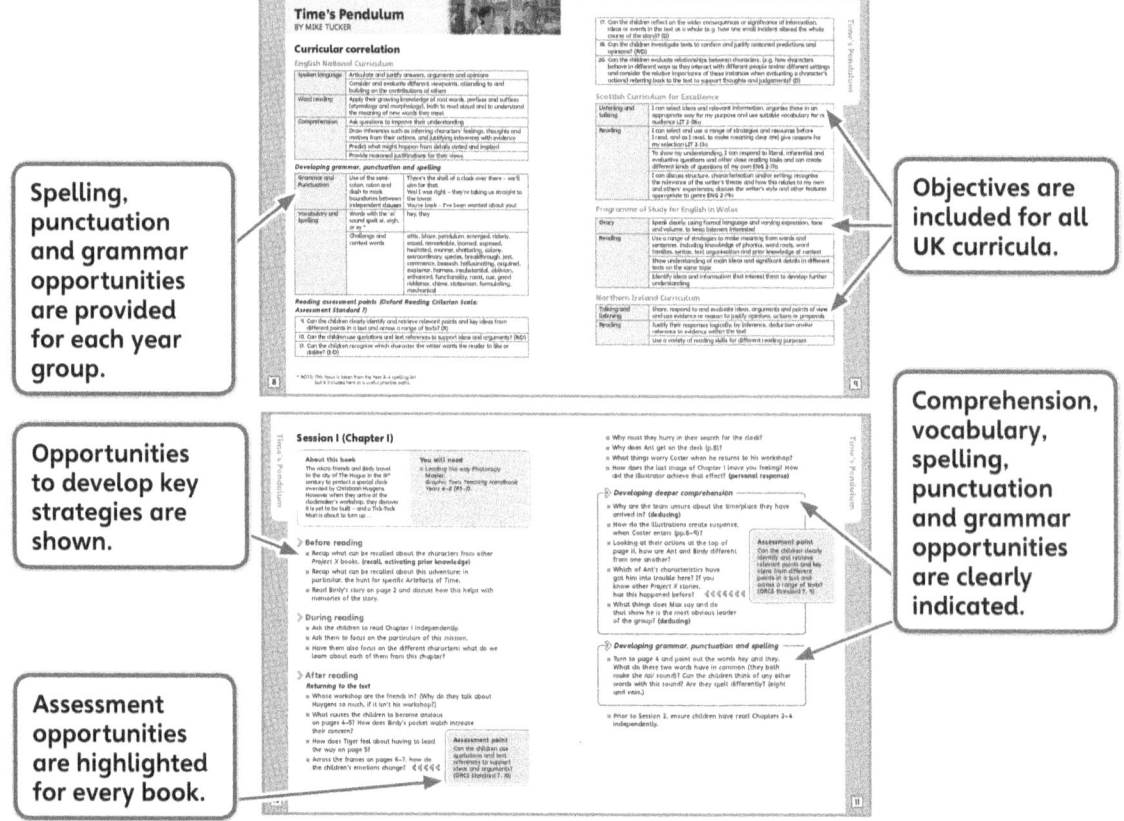

Guided Reading Notes (Oxford Level 18)

The Teaching Handbook

The *Graphic Texts Teaching Handbook for Years 4–6 (P5–7)* offers guidance to show how **Project X *Origins graphic texts*** can be used effectively in guided reading, with a focus on using the integrated artwork and text to develop comprehension skills. There is also guidance on how the books can support building an outstanding reading school, including help in delivering the reading curriculum, assessing reading level and engaging parents and carers. Photocopiable resources to support follow-up work are provided for every book as well as some generic ones.

Professional Development

Getting the most out of guided reading

Oxford Owl has a number of Professional Development resources to support teachers:

- Professional Development films from Lindsay Pickton, Nikki Gamble and James Clements, which include how to run **Project X *Origins*** guided reading sessions and the features of good guided reading.
- School Improvement Pathways and Reports which help you create a whole-school plan for guided reading.

Raising boys' achievement

- The *Let's Get Boys Reading and Writing Handbook* offers ideas and practical advice on how to improve boys' reading.

Home-school links

Project X *Origins graphic texts* supports the vital link between home and school with guidance on engaging parents and carers. In addition, every book includes notes to support parents and carers should children wish to take these books home. More support for parents/carers is available online at *Oxford Owl*.

Jabberwocky and other poems (Oxford Level 18)

Structure and components

Year	Book Band	Oxford Level	Character fiction	Classics	Poetry	Non-fiction	Teaching Resources	
Year 4/ P5	Grey	14	Chasing Birdy	The Wind in the Willows	Pelican Chorus	Great Artists	Guided Reading Notes	
	Dark Blue	15	Time Stealer	The Jungle Book	If	Great Inventors	Guided Reading Notes	
Year 5/ P6		16	The Sands of Deception	The Secret Garden	I Wandered Lonely as a Cloud	Great Naturalists	Guided Reading Notes	
	Dark Red	17	The Jurchen Recruits	Treasure Island	The Pied Piper of Hamelin	Great Space Explorers	Guided Reading Notes	Teaching Handbook
		18	Time's Pendulum	Alice's Adventures in Wonderland	Jabberwocky and other poems	Great Scientists	Guided Reading Notes	
Year 6/ P7	Dark Red+	19	Antarctic Ambush	The Call of the Wild	The Raven	Great Engineers	Guided Reading Notes	
		20	Time Runs Out	Oliver Twist	For the Fallen and other poems	Great Pioneers	Guided Reading Notes	

The reading books in more depth

Project X *Origins graphic texts* is perfect for developing comprehension skills. Developed by experts, it offers children a rich variety of reading matter across fiction, poetry and non-fiction genres.

⟩⟩ Character fiction

The Project X *Origins graphic texts* series includes seven brand-new fiction stories, with a thrilling new adventure, featuring the ever-popular **Project X** characters Max, Cat, Ant and Tiger. Many children will already have developed relationships with the four heroes and their special watches that allow them to shrink to micro-size, and this familiarity will ease them into the challenge of increasingly complex graphic storytelling. Moreover, seeing these characters in this different, dynamic form, has the potential to seize children's attention, and hold it over time. Although the familiar characters provide an instant pull for existing readers, each story stands alone so children who are unfamiliar with the **Project X** world won't find themselves at a disadvantage: at the front of each book there is an overview of the plot, ensuring that children will be up to speed before starting to read.

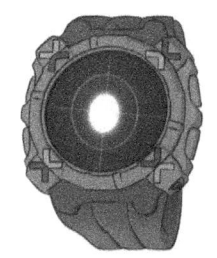

In the first book (*Chasing Birdy*), a new, unsociable, girl arrives at school (named Birdy). After school, Birdy runs off. Sure that something odd is going on, the micro-friends follow her across town to the highest point in Greenville – the roof of the library. As storm clouds gather, Birdy starts up an odd-looking machine (her Escape Wheel) and a swirling vortex emerges. The friends are pulled into the vortex after her and find themselves transported to another place and time. Before Birdy has time to explain, a strange, malignant, robot (a Tick-Tock Man) appears. After the friends save Birdy from its clutches, she eventually trusts them enough to let them know what's going on …

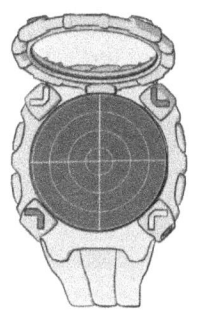

In the year 2099, the head of a powerful communications and cybernetics company, Kalvin Spearhead, has designed a time machine to protect the people of Earth from a massive asteroid that will destroy it. He claims he can save humanity – but Birdy and her gran (the head scientist at Spearhead's company) aren't so sure. Gran is in favour of trying to find an alternative solution to stopping the asteroid that won't risk changing the past. Birdy has taken it upon herself to put a stop to Spearhead's plan – she must travel back in time to collect the seven Artefacts of Time he needs to complete his machine. Unfortunately, Spearhead's robotic army are also after the Artefacts of Time …

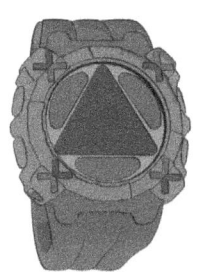

Over the following six books, the four friends try to help Birdy find the Artefacts of Time before the Tick-Tock Men and save future Earth.

Classics

The classics within this series have been devised with a passion for the original material but with a contemporary look and feel which makes it accessible to today's children. For some children, the inherent 'fun' element in a graphic text enables them to engage with the stories, whereas the original versions may feel daunting due to the demands of the vocabulary and the references that can appear archaic to a modern child. It is frequently the case that the graphic medium provides a route into the originals; these are, after all, classics for a reason. It may be that the graphic version remains the favoured one, just as some people prefer a particular film adaptation of *Oliver Twist* or a contemporary re-imagining of *The Jungle Book* to the original.

Some children may, of course, come to these graphic versions having already read the originals, and it is always fascinating to discuss their preferences and how the images in their own minds differed from the illustrated representations. The comparison of the original novel with the contemporary graphic version may be taken further through the exploration of film/television adaptations. Similarities and differences between audio-visual and illustrated art forms may be teased out, enhancing comprehension of the original story in an enjoyable and memorable way.

Poetry

The graphic retelling of classic poetry has many similarities to that of classic novels, but there are some additional elements to consider. A much greater proportion of the language of poetry tends toward the figurative and the graphic form can help the reader to make sense of, often complex, metaphors. As well as helping to lead the narrative through the text, the images used in the graphic form help to make what otherwise might be inaccessible content, accessible. There is a great deal to consider in how the illustrator chooses to represent the imagery of the poem on the page. How do children react to these choices, and how do these choices affect comprehension of figurative language? If they read (or heard) the poem in text-only form initially, how did their visualizations and understanding compare with the pictorial form? Having children produce their own dramatic freeze-frame or artwork in response to hearing the poem, prior to viewing the graphic version, can provoke even deeper engagement and analysis. If, on the other hand, the graphic version is encountered first, it is powerful to explore the extent to which it helps their comprehension of the original, including a better understanding of authorial intent.

The following table details the individual poems included within the theme- or author-linked collections:

Year	Book Band	Oxford Level	Title	'Theme' of collection	Poems included
4	Grey	14	The Pelican Chorus *and other poems*	Funny/nonsense poems	• 'The Pelican Chorus' by Edward Lear • 'There was an Old Man …' by Edward Lear • 'The Duel' by Eugene Field • 'Mr Toad' by Kenneth Grahame • 'My Shadow' by Robert Louis Stevenson
		15	If *and other poems*	Poems by Rudyard Kipling	• 'If' • 'The Secret of the Machines' • 'The Way through the Woods' • 'Thorkild's Song'
5	Dark Blue	16	I Wandered Lonely as a Cloud *and other poems*	Nature poems	• 'I Wandered Lonely as a Cloud' by William Wordsworth • 'The Wind' by Robert Louis Stevenson • 'Pirate Story' by Robert Louis Stevenson • 'Bed in Summer' by Robert Louis Stevenson • 'The World Below the Brine' by Walt Whitman • 'Past, Present, Future' by Emily Brontë • 'The Falling Star' by Sara Teasdale
		17	The Pied Piper of Hamelin	Narrative poem by Robert Browning	• *The Pied Piper of Hamelin*
6	Dark Red	18	Jabberwocky *and other poems*	Poems by Lewis Carroll	• 'Jabberwocky' • 'How Doth the Little Crocodile' • 'The Walrus and the Carpenter' • 'Humpty Dumpty's Recitation'
	Dark Red+	19	The Raven *and other poems*	Animal poems	• 'The Raven' by Edgar Alan Poe • 'The Tiger' by William Blake • 'Snake' by D. H. Lawrence • 'The Eagle' by Alfred, Lord Tennyson • 'The Snail' by William Cowper
		20	For the Fallen *and other poems*	War poems	• 'For the Fallen' by Laurence Binyon • 'Dulce et Decorum Est' by Wilfred Owen • 'An Irish Airman Forsees his Own Death' by W. B. Yeats • 'Here Dead We Lie' by A.E. Housman • 'To Germany' by Charles Hamilton Sorley • 'Dirge for Two Veterans' by Walt Whitman • 'I Saw Old General at Bay' by Walt Whitman • 'The Charge of the Light Brigade' by Alfred, Lord Tennyson

Non-fiction

Project X *Origins graphic texts* includes enlightening and enriching cross-curricular non-fiction, from the worlds of history, the arts, science and geography, in the form of retellings of the biographies of significant figures in the history of human progress. Just as the graphic medium may ease some children in to encountering awe-inspiring stories and poems that might otherwise feel out of their reach, so it will help them connect with subject matter that might appear dry or unappealing in traditional non-fiction form. The immediacy and inherent humanity of the artwork – the fact that illustrators can show the emotions these figures may have experienced – opens the way to a different kind of classic: one that will enhance children's knowledge of history and science. The books also include more traditional non-fiction elements – contents page, text-only pages with bullet-pointed facts, glossary and index.

The following table details the 'Greats' included within each non-fiction book:

Year	Book Band	Oxford Level	Title	'Greats' included
4	Grey	14	Great Artists	Leonardo da Vinci, Claude Monet, Edvard Munch, Pablo Picasso, Barbara Hepworth
	Dark Blue	15	Great Inventors	Archimedes, Johannes Gutenberg, Alexander Graham Bell, Thomas Edison, Garrett Morgan
5		16	Great Naturalists	Jane Goodall, John James Audubon, Karl von Frisch, Mary Anning, Kathleen Drew-Baker, David Douglas
	Dark Red	17	Great Space Explorers	Shi Shen and Gan De, Aristarchus of Samos, Hipparchus of Nicaea, Claudius Ptolemy, Nicolaus Copernicus, Galileo Galilei, Williamina Stevens Fleming
6		18	Great Scientists	Isaac Newton, Carl Linnaeus, Michael Faraday, Marie Curie, Albert Einstein, Alexander Fleming, Alan Turing
	Dark Red+	19	Great Engineers	Imhotep, Apollodorus of Damascus, Isambard Kingdom Brunel, Emily Roebling, Karl Benz, Sergei Korolev
		20	Great Pioneers	Pioneers of television, Emmeline Pankhurst, Amelia Earhart, Frank Whittle, Clarence Birdseye, Jacques Piccard, Nelson Mandela

About the series advisors

Project X *Origins graphic texts* has been developed with a team of advisors, experts in the fields of education and graphic texts.

Dave Gibbons (Series Editor)

Dave Gibbons established himself in underground comics and fanzines in Britain before becoming a frequent contributor to the seminal *2000 AD*, illustrating *Harlem Heroes*, *Dan Dare* and co-creating *Rogue Trooper*. Since then, he has drawn and written for most comics publishers on both sides of the Atlantic. His work has encompassed *Dr Who*, *Superman*, *Batman*, *Green Lantern*, *Captain America*, *Dr Strange*, *The Hulk*, *Predator* and *Aliens*. With writer Frank Miller he co-created *Give Me Liberty* and the *Martha Washington* series. *Watchmen*, his collaboration with writer Alan Moore, is the best-selling graphic novel ever published and became a major motion picture. His autobiographical graphic novel *The Originals* won an Eisner Award in 2005. His recent work has included *Kingsman: The Secret Service*, with Mark Millar.

In 2015, Dave was appointed the first ever Comics Laureate by the charity CLAw (Comics Literacy Awareness); part of his remit in this biennial post is to spearhead campaigns to improve child literacy in the UK by using comics and graphic novels. In June of the same year, he was awarded an honorary doctorate by the University Of Dundee in recognition of his achievements in comics.

Lindsay Pickton and Christine Chen

Lindsay Pickton found reading tedious as a young child and was uninterested by the limited range of books available in the classroom. He started reading comics around the age of seven, but it was *2000 AD* (featuring Judge Dredd) that turned him into a reader. Within a year or so, he was getting sci-fi and adventure novels from the library … but he never stopped reading *2000 AD*. He discovered 'weightier' graphic texts in his teens, and still counts *Watchmen* and *V for Vendetta* amongst his favourite novels.

Christine Chen grew up in an artistic household in which English was an additional language, with Chinese parents originating from India. Her home-reading diet consisted solely of comics and graphic texts. Along with her sisters and brothers, she relished sharing traditional British comics – often having arguments about which one was best: *Whizzer and Chips*, *Dandy*, *Beano* or *Buster*! The siblings also loved the drama of American *Archie* comics and were fascinated by their father's graphic novels. Graphic texts started and sustained their reading, contributing not only to their language acquisition but also to their love of reading and eventual academic successes.

Both Lindsay and Christine graduated in English and became teachers before becoming independent Primary Education Advisors. In this role they are keen to instil in children the passion for reading and writing that they found to be so enriching and life-changing.

Mel Gibson

Mel Gibson is a Senior Lecturer at Northumbria University where she specializes in teaching and research relating to children and young people, literature and media. She has a huge interest in visual literacies.

Mel is a National Teaching Fellow as well as a comics, and graphic novels scholar and consultant. In addition to her research in this area she has run training and promotional events about comics and graphic novels for libraries, schools and other organizations since 1993.

The importance of graphic texts

The National Curriculum speaks of reading as opening 'a treasure-house of wonder and joy' (p.14). For this to ensue, we must nurture in children a genuine desire to read; for young readers to be hooked by their reading experiences. Comics and graphic novels are very often the texts that hook children in this way, but some adults – parents and teachers among them – may have a sneaking suspicion that this is due to the graphic form being in some way 'easy'.

There are a number of things in this wariness that are worth unpicking. Firstly, the notion that it is somehow wrong to choose to read something that's easily accessible needs contesting: do we as adults always choose 'challenging' reading material? Is it truly the case that only challenging texts can 'improve' us as people? Secondly, the idea that a reading material is 'easy' just because it presents itself pictorially and with fewer words: many highly-literate, educated, intelligent adults enjoy and learn from graphic texts; many graphic texts are seriously challenging.

Reading is not just word reading; this is obvious, but it bears repeating, and often. The development of real comprehension (reading for pleasure and purpose) is the goal; word reading is a means to this end. The special challenge presented by graphic texts is that, with reduced word counts, the focus is placed all the more acutely on comprehension, with a heavy emphasis on interpretation and inference from visuals.

Oliver Twist (Oxford Level 20)

This is not to deny the instant appeal of the graphic medium. It is clear that children are growing up in an increasingly visually-enhanced world which may go some way to explain the draw of graphic texts. However, children loved comics for decades before computer-gaming and televisions in bedrooms became commonplace, so perhaps our fascination with graphic texts lies in the fact that human beings learn to read facial expressions and body language (whether that be face-to-face, on screen, or as images in books) long before they learn to read words.

The apparent accessibility of the graphic medium may also enable the introduction of high-level concepts and themes, almost as if cognitive challenge sneaks up on those expecting entertainment (though, of course, the two are not mutually exclusive). Many children benefit from this: perhaps most obviously, those (often boys) who are ready for complex themes, but don't think reading is 'for them'; children with English as an additional language whose language development is aided by the visuals; children who prefer more succinct text; avid readers who are ready for a different kind of reading experience. Traditionally, graphic texts have been categorized as 'for boys' but the girl-appeal of these books shouldn't be underestimated. In recent years, many graphic texts have been created and published by women, and increasingly feature female protagonists in strong roles. While the action and adventure elements of graphic texts may be said to appeal to the boy stereotype, reading people and making inferences about feelings may reach out to the 'typical' girl; graphic texts give children of both sexes exposure to the above, hopefully going some way to blur these historic distinctions.

There is now an established tradition of presenting classic literature to children through the graphic text format, not least with many of Shakespeare's plays. The comic-strip depiction of tales that might otherwise appear to be inaccessible to some young or insecure readers has enabled early exploration and enjoyment of our literary heritage.

Alice's Adventures in Wonderland (Oxford Level 18)

But there's much more to graphic texts than simply retelling classics. Looking back, it can be seen that they have established their own place in our literary heritage. *Maus*, created by Art Spiegelman from 1980–1991, deals unflinchingly with the Holocaust and is a genuine modern classic, winning the Pulitzer Prize in 1992. *Watchmen*, in which Alan Moore and Dave Gibbons present an alternative 20th-century history, was recognized in *Time* magazine's list of the 100 best English language novels since 1923. (Interestingly, both *Maus* and *Watchmen* were originally serialized as comics before being bound as novels – much like Dickens' great works.) While these are both more adult texts, their standing does highlight the gravitas that the graphic form can achieve. Comic-strip tales retelling and dramatizing events from the world wars continue to be an intrinsic part of our culture. It appears that there is something about the graphic depiction of people and situations that lends itself to exploring the most potent themes. We can think of the imagery on Ancient Greek vases and the walls of Egyptian tombs – even Paleolithic cave paintings – which tell stories of importance that can move us over the millennia.

Graphic texts and the National Curriculum

The emphasis in the National Curriculum for England on reading for pleasure, and the potential role that graphic texts have in this, has already been expressed, and it is crucial that the goal of developing children's reading for pleasure is never far from our minds: children who enjoy reading read frequently, and seem to do better in all academic subjects as a consequence – even maths.[1]

Guidance on how an increase in reading for pleasure might be achieved, or what it might look like, may be found within the National Curriculum programmes of study (PoS), with strong reference to an 'increasingly wide range' of reading material, and 'books that are structured in different ways', both of which may be said to implicitly include graphic texts.

Those reading foci that explicitly focus on understanding the exploration of 'the meaning of words in context', 'inferring characters' feelings, thoughts and motives from their actions', and 'identifying how language, structure and presentation contribute to meaning' (Y5/6; there are similarly-worded points in Y3/4)– all easily lend themselves to the use of graphic texts generally. Emphasis on 'our literary heritage' also fits well with **Project X Origins graphic texts**, particularly the classic fiction, which is also perfect for 'making comparisons within and across books/texts'. The historical/scientific biographies lend themselves to 'retriev(ing) … information from non-fiction' and 'distinguish(ing) between … fact and opinion', as well as the requirements of other curricular areas to learn about key figures from our cultural and scientific heritage. Finally, the graphic representations of classic poems support the 'learning by heart' and performance of poetry – potentially including the graphic-friendly 'intonation, tone, volume and action'.

More generally, it is hard to find points from the PoS that *don't* work well with these graphic texts; but the keys are enjoyment and range. For children who can read, but don't yet enjoy it, graphic texts are often an excellent help into that 'treasure house of wonder and joy'; for children who read keenly but whose choice of material is limited, the breadth of the **Project X Origins graphic texts** range, combined with the instant accessibility inherent in the form, may open up new worlds.

> More detail about how **Project X** fits in with the National Curriculum in England can be found on page 38.

The Pelican Chorus and other poems (Oxford Level 14)

---

[1] Sullivan and Brown, 'Social inequalities in cognitive scores at age 16: The role of reading', Institute of Education (2013)

Using graphic texts for guided reading

Guided reading is a fantastic tool for developing comprehension through small group discussion. By Year 4/Primary 5, the great majority of children have at least reasonable word-reading skills and so it makes sense to focus on guided reading as one of the main reading strategies in the classroom. Given that graphic texts are comparatively light on word count and yet require high levels of comprehension, they are well-suited to the guided reading approach. Discussion around the comprehension of graphic texts will, of course, encompass the interpretation of illustrated content; stories and characters are developed pictorially and there are always inferences to be made from facial expressions, body language and other elements that are not verbalized. But this doesn't mean that the words are not important; on the contrary, rather like poetry, the relative scarcity of language necessitates greater consideration of vocabulary choices. Indeed, the artwork often scaffolds the introduction of advanced vocabulary; but even the apparently simpler words can be laden with meaning.

The true value of guided reading is in the peer dialogue around interpretations and how inferences are made from what's on the page. The guided reading process allows the teacher to facilitate children in formulating their own, and building on each others', thoughts about the text, always expecting these to be anchored in evidence rather than pure speculation.

Time Runs Out (Oxford Level 20)

Graphic texts appear to automatically lend themselves to the social aspect of reading and the shared enjoyment of texts; perhaps this is enhanced by the fact that everyone is seeing the same characters in the same settings, making it more akin to watching a film or a play. When reading a text-based story, we construct our own unique visuals, making it a more individual experience (although this, of course, leads to valuable discussion about our often differing interpretations). When a story is told largely visually, the impact is rapid – almost instant – in its effect on a reader's emotions; moreover, the reader may be simultaneously marvelling at the artistry that has achieved that impact. This experience appears to facilitate a shared appreciation, and therefore guided reading that isn't merely good or even great, but potentially joyful – even when the subject matter is serious.

Good guided reading practice

- Every guided reading session should feel pleasurable, like the sort of book group that many adults attend for both enjoyment and the encouragement of greater breadth of reading.

- Good guided reading often requires that children pre-read the part of the book to be explored in the group session – perhaps with a very broad focus question, such as, "How does Max change through the first chapters?", or, "How do you know what Buck is feeling in each scene?" – in order that they are ready to move rapidly beyond literal understanding when the group comes together, allowing more time for discussion. Taking turns to read aloud in a group is seldom very effective for the development of comprehension, and this is particularly true for graphic texts where so much of the 'reading' is told through the artwork and is therefore more of an 'internal' process, often requiring rereading to digest the narrative and to ensure understanding.

- You may have a specific learning point to teach from the National Curriculum programmes of study (PoS), but if you tell the children this is what the session is about, then the session is no longer about their own reading, and it certainly isn't about their enjoyment. Successful guided reading sessions feel like a natural conversation, in which author technique is explored as it arises.

- Ask open questions so children have the opportunity to develop their own views. Then with talk partners and/or in groups, prompt children to expand on their own and each others' contributions: 'That's interesting. Say some more about that …', 'Would you agree with what she said?', 'What makes you think that?', 'How do you know?'. Ensure you listen to children's responses and require that they expand upon them, with evidence, It is important that unfounded speculations are challenged: it is simply not the case that all answers are 'right' in some way! To find out more about the importance of talk in guided reading, please go to page 27.

- Build in time for each child to generate a question about the text that they want the rest of the group to answer. This provides invaluable insights into what the children observe and understand, while also being fun!

For more advice on getting the most out of guided reading turn to page 25.

Key considerations for using graphic texts

Approaching the text

A stimulating way to capture children's interest when first approaching a text together can be to choose a frame that represents a key moment from the story and have children articulate what led to this point and what might ensue.

Cinematic analysis

Using graphic texts presents some unique challenges and opportunities to the guided development of comprehension, and many of these are quite closely related to the analysis performed by students of cinema: the choices made in the visual presentation of frames, the relationship between this and the words used, and the movement between scenes. Consider the point of view the illustrator has brought to certain frames. What is the impact of a close-up, a long distance shot, an overhead or an upward-looking angle? What has been put in the foreground/background? How is the scene 'lit'? From which character's viewpoint are we experiencing the scene, or is the scene presented to us as external observers? Children need to be made aware that the illustrator and author have made these sorts of decisions with great thoughtfulness regarding the impact on the reader. Every detail in every frame has a purpose, with a literal or symbolic meaning. The real question is always: how do these choices carry our experience of the story along?

Artwork style

Illustrators have different styles; sometimes a particular illustrator is chosen because their style suits the material; also, some illustrators may adapt their style for different effects. Have children consider the appropriateness of the style to the subject matter or atmosphere.

The palette used by an illustrator is always worth noting: have they gone for realism, hyper-realism, romantic, or sombre and subdued? Sometimes stark changes in colouring may indicate turning points in a story, shifts in mood, or transitions in location or time, or one point of view to another.

Changes in time

Graphic texts can have a distinctive way of playing with time; for example, through narrative inserts containing adverbials, such as, 'Later ...', or the leaping of time and place from one frame to the next. It is worth investigating this. How much time has passed? How much space has been covered? What's the duration of, say, a single page? The same number of frames can represent seconds, minutes, weeks or decades, so compare how time passes on different pages. And, where they occur, how have any flashbacks been signalled, stylistically?

What happens between frames

Notice what isn't said and what isn't depicted, especially between frames. There is often much to be inferred in the transitions. As Dave Gibbons himself explains, it's the 'white spaces' between the images where the comprehension/links have to happen.

Sub-plots

In more complex stories, look out for how sub-plots complement the main story, and how they are handled so that a reader doesn't become confused by events running alongside each other. Why does the sub-plot matter? What would happen if it were removed?

Characters

Look closely at what characters say, the specific words they use and the way they say them – the facial expressions and body language represented, as well as the point of view. How a character is portrayed visually has an impact on how we receive and interpret the language they use, and therefore the extent to which we sympathize with them. Are the words accompanied with a tear, a smirk or a grimace?

Viewpoint

Notice also the relationship between said dialogue and any narrative inserts; is there some conflict, or different viewpoint, between the narrator and certain characters?

The Wind in the Willows (Oxford Level 14)

Progression and comprehension in graphic texts

It is vital that the general diet of texts children encounter through Key Stage 2 develops to meet their maturing appetite, knowledge and skill. As children become more experienced and accomplished readers, and as our expectations for them increase, so texts should become more complex and more rich. The **Project X *Origins graphic texts*** have been structured to reflect, as well as challenge, expected Key Stage 2 progression in reading comprehension.

Information retrieval is a deceptively problematic skill, and it is important to keep practising it with gradually more challenging texts: keep checking that children 'get' what is going on, and have them recast their newly acquired understanding in different ways; presentations, drama (including manipulation of point-of-view), and the use of the age-appropriate organizational formats provided within the photocopiable masters. These, are all examples of cognitively demanding applications that require reading retrieval. While younger readers will be equipped to undertake retellings of stories (fictional or otherwise), as they become more proficient, we should plan opportunities for them to exercise the higher-order skills of summary – for example, précising stories or information – as well as evaluating the success of any intended impact on readers. What in Year 4 may be expressed as, "What's the intended purpose and how successful is this?" can, by Year 6, become, "What techniques have the author and illustrator used to convey this, e.g. humour?"

While constantly revisiting and extending retrieval, there must also be an on-going emphasis on inference; this is an area of persisting difficulty for very many children and one that it is necessary to overcome if a child is to progress in the reading curriculum, as well as in their own capacity to read for purpose and pleasure. This is one area to which graphic texts are perfectly suited: the more mature the text, the greater the requirement for inference from the artwork; the thoughts and feelings behind characters' actions and expressions become less transparent and the unpicking of these through group discussion will lead to deeper inferences. Additionally, in upper Key Stage 2, children will be more readily receptive to the meta-language required to discuss the author's craft; how a reader is led to certain interpretations, e.g. whether or not an author chooses to provide a close-up of a character, or the decision behind which perspective to take. By Year 4, most children are more than ready to find clues in visual representations and this can provide a springboard for the development of inferential skills, as well as scaffolding the acquisition of new vocabulary.

The relative scarcity of words in this medium often means that each word packs more of a punch, and this in turn means that there is a great deal of inference to be developed when talking about the vocabulary, as well as the artwork. In upper Key Stage 2, this can be developed into discussion about the absence of certain words and what we might infer from what's not said. As texts become more advanced, moreover, there is greater use of figurative language to match children's growing ability to abstract.

Besides exploring the inferences required by the images and the text separately, there is a wealth of comprehension to be developed in looking at the relationship between the two. Graphic texts are uniquely positioned to provoke discussion around how an author and illustrator balance the interplay between text and artwork.

Themes arising from texts studied through Years 4, 5 and 6 (P5–7) become increasingly mature, with issues growing in complexity. Expect children to more readily take on and discuss themes such as overcoming adversity or fear, and the power of nature, and that of friendship; as this becomes more practised, expect them to identify, unprompted, where these themes emerge, and the viewpoint that the author/illustrator take(s) about them. Alongside this, there will be a growing capacity to notice – and discuss – subplots that may carry themes of their own.

As children move into upper Key Stage 2, the conventions of graphic texts can be explored more explicitly, especially through comparison of different styles.

Great Engineers (Oxford Level 19)

Planning and assessment

Real guided reading is one of the most effective strategies for improving children's comprehension, but, as already stated, pre-planning a list of questions for guided reading sessions can hamper high-quality dialogue and therefore hinder true understanding. The very best use of planning time is getting to know the text so that we are equipped to guide the discussion, challenge misapprehensions and lead children to a more thorough grasp of their reading. By becoming truly familiar with the material, we may thoroughly exploit more of its potential for moving children's reading skills forward, while exciting them about the content and pre-empting the likely stumbling-blocks. Getting to know a text to this depth might seem time-consuming, but it may actually be time-efficient as, once a book is this well-known to you, it is likely that you will be able to use it over multiple sessions with different groups of children; you may even be able to use it in totally different contexts – for example, as a stimulus for an English sequence of work or for PHSE – not just for guided reading.

Obviously, besides knowing the text, you have to know the children: what they currently like and dislike, as well as what they can and can't yet do; formative assessment, in other words. The aforementioned thorough knowledge of the text is extremely useful here, as it will enable you to change the session according to the children's needs.

It is also clearly vital to know what is required, statutorily, by the National Curriculum for England programmes of study (PoS) for the children's year group.

In summary, to successfully a plan a guided reading session, you should:
- know the children and what they need,
- know the texts,
- know the progression through the programmes of study.

For more advice on getting the most out of guided reading turn to page 25.

If these three points are orchestrated thoughtfully, and used to generate a few potential questions, reading progress will happen. 'Thoughtfully' implies that during sessions, teachers genuinely listen to what children actually say, in order to take the discussion from there. The PoS for Years 3 and 4 as well as Years 5 and 6 emphasize 'checking that the book/text makes sense to them' through discussion, and time must be planned for this: ask questions that enable children to demonstrate that they understand what is going on and what the text is about. It's important not to move on until it is clear that children's comprehension is secure, for nothing else will develop without it.

As the PoS for reading comprehension are minimal – designed to focus attention on the essential skills – there is huge scope for spending much more time getting to know a single text and/or revisiting the PoS in a wide variety of contexts, all the time expecting children to improve their responses with this increased practice. It is necessary to plan opportunities for comparison, too – including but not limited to graphic and original versions of a classic.

The reading comprehension PoS are explicit on the discursive aspect of comprehension, including having children ask each other questions, predicting, drawing and justifying inferences. The point that states, 'Participate in discussions about books ... building on their own and others' ideas and challenging views courteously', (Y5/6) encapsulates what a good guided reading session should be, whilst also developing a fundamental life skill. For children to be able to adopt this manner of dialogue, adult modelling will almost always be required, of course.

The true assessment of reading is the extent to which children meet the programmes of study, using many different texts. What the planning and assessment process looks like on a week-by-week basis, and the formats used, are entirely a matter for each school; generally speaking, the less wordy, the better; and when teachers attempt (or are required) to record assessments while leading a guided group, their capacity to listen and guide is hamstrung. Looking at a defined progression – for example, the Oxford Reading Criterion Scale – perhaps at the end of the day or in a lunch break, is an efficient way of logging concisely the ongoing assessment and determining what that group of children need next.

More guidance about how to assess progress with the Oxford Reading Criterion Scale can be found on page 83.

Chasing Birdy (Oxford Level 14)

The fact that children's reading will eventually be assessed in a written test cannot be ignored, and it is important that they are regularly required to express their comprehension in writing. This is not to say that they should sit frequent comprehension papers (too much of this may hamper their enjoyment of reading); rather, the types of written response required by the independent photocopiable masters in this handbook can provide appropriate practice that is also stimulating and engaging. Similarly, having children record their thoughts – formally, or even just on sticky-notes – when pre-reading for a guided reading session, will contribute to their ability to express evidence-based understanding in written form.

Graphic texts are intrinsically suited to the development of reading comprehension (and, frequently, of enjoyment), but as has already been noted, the artwork often scaffolds the acquisition of new vocabulary as well. The PoS for Key Stage 2 have very little to say about word reading, but learning new words is paramount; it may be useful to have children record words that they have conquered (whether in graphic or other texts) and, potentially, have these as an ever-evolving display.

How Project X *Origins* can support building an outstanding reading school

Outstanding reading schools believe in both the importance of developing children's discrete word-reading skills and comprehension, and the need to engender their love of books and reading. They place reading and books at the centre of school life and recognize that being able to read well is a key life skill for all children; and they believe that every child can learn to read, given the right teaching and the right support.

In outstanding reading schools – as with **Project X *Origins*** – great importance is placed on:

- developing children's word-reading skills,
- developing strong comprehension skills, focusing on specific aspects so that over time children develop a repertoire of comprehension strategies,
- motivating 21st-century children to want to read with exciting narratives, engaging characters and fascinating topics.

Project X *Origins* supports every child to become a confident, competent reader – a key part of any outstanding reading school.

Six strategies to build an outstanding reading school

This handbook provides guidance to show how **Project X *Origins*** can support the following strategies to help build an outstanding reading school:

	1	2	3	4	5	6
	Supporting staff	Teaching the reading curriculum	Engaging parents and carers	Developing the reading environment	Targeting resources	Celebrating reading
Project X Origins	Guidance to help get the most out of every guided reading session	Support on using guided reading to meet the needs of the reading curriculum	Support to create a collaborative approach to developing a shared reading culture at home and at school	Advice on creating an effective reading environment	Support to assess and identify readers' needs and choose the right books for each child	Tips to help celebrate the success each child makes and to raise the profile of reading
	page 25	page 32	page 78	page 81	page 83	page 106

▶ Building an Outstanding Reading School

To find out more about the six strategies developed by English advisor and former school leader, James Clements, download your copy of the Oxford School Improvement report at: www.oxfordprimary.co.uk

I. Supporting staff: getting the most out of guided reading

When delivered effectively, guided reading plays a key role in helping children to develop as independent and successful readers. Small-group work, at the centre of guided reading, offers a number of benefits, allowing:

- greater interaction and dialogue between adults and children, and between children
- children to learn collaboratively from one another
- teachers to closely focus objectives on children's specific learning needs.

That is not to say, however, that delivering an effective guided reading session is simple. Here are five areas teachers might wish to consider when setting up and running guided reading sessions:

   a. Organizing groups and differentiating learning
   b. The role of the teacher
   c. The importance of talk
   d. Learning from each other
   e. Balancing the needs of the whole class.

Organizing groups and differentiating learning

From Year 4/P5 through to Year 6/P7, guided reading plays a vital role in developing children's reading skills. As children progress as readers, the structure of guided reading sessions can change to meet the needs of children at every stage of their development.

Small groups organized by reading level work well if the text is closely matched to the children's needs as developing readers as well as allowing children opportunities to consolidate previously learned skills. However, even within these groups there can be some variation in children's reading ability and their precise development needs – working in a small group allows time for direct teaching with each child to encourage and monitor their understanding, targeting questions and addressing any misconceptions.

For guided reading sessions, consider placing children in groups of approximately four to six children of similar reading ability. Select books that are at the appropriate instructional level for each group – for guided reading, this means that children should be able to read the text with 90 per cent accuracy. Children will progress at different speeds so it is important to review these groupings regularly to respond to the progress each child makes.

> *Targeting resources*
>
> Guidance on assessing the level each child is working at, choosing the right book for each group and making ongoing assessments can be found on page 83.

The role of the teacher

As the word 'guided' indicates, the role of the teacher is vital. In guided reading the teacher can lead with direct instruction, the children's learning can be 'scaffolded' and the learning focus made explicit. In guided reading the level of challenge can be finely matched to the needs of the children within the group and the teacher can support children to tackle themes, ideas, questions that might be beyond them individually.

Guided reading provides opportunities to model examples of the skills children need to develop in order to progress as readers, for example comprehension strategies they can use to understand texts of increasing complexity. It is important to remember that the teacher's role in guiding reading is to give children just enough help to support their learning and encourage independent and collaborative problem-solving skills, reducing children's level of dependency and helping to ensure they become successful independent readers.

It may be useful to explore the level of interaction and communication within existing guided reading sessions, using a simple model, such as the one shown below, to consider whether children can be encouraged to work more collaboratively.

Limited interaction between children

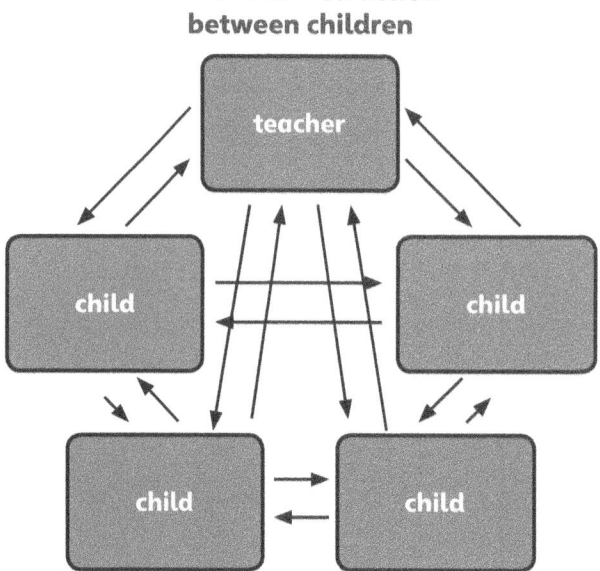

Increased interaction between children

⚅ The importance of talk

Effective guided reading sessions give every child the opportunity to speak frequently, contributing to discussion and answering questions. It is an excellent way to support the development of children's spoken language which is crucial to learning; it underpins the development of thinking and allows children to develop their understanding and confidence.

The small-group structure of guided reading means that each child has an opportunity to speak, listen and then respond, something that can be difficult to organize within a whole-class situation. In addition, these general principles should also be borne in mind:

Do	Possible techniques
Ask questions that will challenge children cognitively as well as asking them to recall simple facts or events.	• Use open ended questions. • Use the full range of 'question' words – 'why' and 'how', as well as 'when', 'where', 'who' and 'what'. • Encourage speculation and exploration by prompting with phrases such as 'What if …?' or 'Imagine that …' or 'I wonder if …'
Encourage children to give extended answers.	• Prompt children to extend their replies by using phrases such as 'tell me more' and/or positive cues such as nodding. • Respond by asking them why they think what they do. How do they know? What's their evidence? • Respond by elaborating on what a child has said by giving a personal example from your own experience and then encouraging them to do the same. • Pause before responding. An extended wait time will often encourage further elaboration.
Give children time to formulate their ideas and views.	• Tell children they have half a minute of 'thinking time'. • Ask them to respond to a 'talk partner' initially. This gives them a chance to rehearse their ideas and also encourages all children to respond. • Use 'think, pair, share'.
Provide models of the patterns of language and the subject vocabulary to be used.	• Ensure children have plenty of opportunities to hear fluent speech. Read aloud to them from the text, talk to them, let them listen to media resources. • Discuss the meanings of words. • Offer oral sentence starters/sentence patterns. • Provide 'talk frames' as a prompt for longer talk activities.
Expect children to speak so that everyone can hear and understand.	• Ask children to repeat what they have said if necessary rather than always repeating or rephrasing it for them. • Get other children to ask for clarification/elaboration rather than reformulating what children have said.
Encourage dialogue and discussion.	• Cue alternative responses using phrases such as 'What do others think?' • Invite other children to respond/question – 'Would anyone like to ask X a question?' • Offer a challenging view – 'Supposing someone said …'

a Learning from each other

Guided reading sessions give children the opportunity to listen and learn from their peers – they can communicate their own ideas and learn from the knowledge and ideas of others in the group. Children can act as an influence on each other's reading too, providing a motivating audience during reading aloud and a possible model for expressive reading when listening.

It is important to stress that although reading with fluency, expression and intonation are important, guided reading is not being used properly if it is merely used as time for children to practise reading aloud in turn. This is particularly true of graphic texts which offer a different reading experience. Children need more time to internalize what's going on and much of this would be lost if read aloud as a group or in pairs. When undertaking guided reading with **Project X *Origins graphic texts***, children should be encouraged to read prior to the session, or independently within the session, before tackling comprehension questions.

Reading partners should be encouraged to discuss the books they share – what they thought of them, what they learned, and any questions they have. This will help build a culture in which children see reading as a social and pleasurable activity. You could encourage reading partners to share their discussion with the guided reading group or the rest of the class depending on when the reading takes place.

Providing children with the prompt sheet on the opposite page will help to scaffold discussions between reading partners.

Reading partner prompts for graphic texts

Before reading
- Look at the book with your partner.
- Discuss what you think it will be about. For example:
    - What do you already know about the story or topic?
    - What can you find out from the cover image and blurb?
- Listen and reply to your partner's ideas.

During reading
- You could share the reading between you – e.g. one person reading one character's speech bubbles, and the other person reading another character's.
- Alternatively, you could both read the whole text independently.

After reading
- Tell each other what you thought of the book.
    - What did you enjoy?
    - What did you find out?
    - What questions do you have?
- Listen and reply to your partner's ideas.

Balancing the needs of the whole class

For guided reading to be as effective as it can be, it is important that it is not only the guided reading group working with the teacher that is actively engaged in learning or consolidating previous learning, but the rest of the class too. There is no single correct way of organizing guided reading and many schools that use a guided reading model to successfully teach reading have many different ways of organizing their sessions and the rest of the class. These vary widely from school to school and even across different year groups, as older children are likely to be capable of more complex independent activities. There are no set rules for the organization but the table below outlines some examples of different models that have proven effective.

Model	Notes
The carousel	Children are organized into groups by reading ability. Over the course of a week, groups move around to undertake a range of different reading activities, including one guided reading session with the teacher. Other activities are likely to include some follow-up work based on the text read with the teacher, a free choice or focused reading task, a word-level task and perhaps an ICT or listening task. **The benefit:** children cover a number of different activities over a week, each with a different learning focus. **The downside:** it can be complicated to organize, children have to have a good level of independence while the teacher works with one group and the independent activities need to be meaningful rather than 'time-fillers' for guided reading to be as effective as possible.
Whole-class task	Children are organized into groups by reading ability. One group works with the teacher each day while the other children carry out a whole-class task, such as reading, undertaking an activity linked to the text they've read with the teacher or a discrete word-level task. **The benefit:** it is relatively quick and easy to organize and can be effective if there is an objective the whole class would benefit from working on. **The downside:** differentiation is possible but must be planned carefully so that children understand and can carry out the task independently, without support from the teacher.
An ongoing project	Children are organized into groups by reading ability. One group works with the teacher each day while the other groups carry out an ongoing, independent task. This approach can be used with older classes who can work well independently. Ongoing projects that schools have used have included producing a class poetry anthology, with children choosing poems and writing about them; or classes writing their own non-fiction texts. **The benefit:** children are carrying out meaningful tasks when they're not with the teacher, consolidating their learning and producing outcomes without a great deal of teacher input before each session. **The downside:** it can be difficult to organize and requires a high level of motivation and self-discipline from the class.

Independent tasks for guided reading

Project X Origins Handbooks and Guided Reading Notes contain a variety of resources to help ensure independent activities are meaningful and support active learning and further develop children's knowledge and understanding. It is important to allow time at the end of any independent activities for a plenary, encouraging the class to share in each other's learning.

Once familiar, these strategies can be used independently by readers both within and beyond guided reading sessions. In addition, below are some alternative independent activities that can be used to engage pupils and further develop their reading ability.

Activity	Learning Focus
Writing task linked to the text, e.g. writing in role as a character from the text children have been reading (letters, diary extract etc.)	Children can demonstrate their understanding and the key knowledge they've acquired through imaginative and creative responses
Sequencing activities	Although used more frequently for younger children, for older children this can help with comprehension and reflection on longer stories and texts
Oral retellings/drama work around stories	Supports recall of the story and development of language
Rewriting the text with a different focus (e.g. writing a story as a play script or from the perspective of a different character)	Supports deeper comprehension, recall of the story and development of key vocabulary
Specific word-level activities (e.g. matching or identifying rhyming words, tasks consolidating specific phonemes, using comparatives)	Supports consolidation of key word-reading objectives and provides an assessment opportunity
Comprehension questions on the text they have read in the session	An assessment opportunity and supports children to articulate their ideas
Reading ready for the next session working with the teacher	For children who are accomplished word readers, this means the entire session with the teacher can be spent on discussion and developing comprehension
Using a dictionary to find the meaning of vocabulary linked to text	Supports vocabulary and developing and the use of dictionaries
Writing book reviews/keeping a reading diary	Supports children to reflect on the books they've read, develop their own taste in books and demonstrate their understanding of the text they've read
Producing storyboards of texts	This can help older children with comprehension and reflection on longer stories and texts
Using a role-play area based on the texts read	Supports rehearsing and exploring language and themes in text studied and encourages empathy with characters
Preparing presentations or notes for discussions on issues raised by the text	Supports rehearsing and exploring language and themes in text studied
Independent reading for pleasure	Provides the opportunity to read for enjoyment
Independent reading for a purpose (e.g. finding key information from a non-fiction text, identifying new or interesting words)	Develops reading for purpose and locating information within a text
Listening to or making recordings of texts	Supports comprehension, develops reading for pleasure and provides a model for fluency

2. Teaching the reading curriculum

Outstanding reading schools use every opportunity there is across the curriculum to help children develop as readers; guided reading can play an important role in the whole-school provision for reading, providing opportunities for children to progress and develop the key competencies they need to become confident and skilled independent readers.

Whole-school

Phonics

Skills/Knowledge coverage
- Develop phonic knowledge and word reading
- Build foundations for later fluency and reading for pleasure
- Develop spelling

Notes
Phonics, word reading and a good knowledge of the common exception words is the starting point for reading. Without being able to read, it is very difficult for children to access the wide range of books that will develop their love of reading.

Whole-class English lessons

Skills/Knowledge coverage
- Develop and apply phonic knowledge and skills to read most words quickly and accurately
- Develop comprehension
- Develop knowledge about a range of texts, genres and authors
- Develop reading for pleasure
- Participate in discussions about books
- Develop grammar, punctuation, vocabulary and spelling

Notes
In many schools whole-class teaching is at the core of the reading curriculum. Reading and discussing books in lessons and using them as a stimulus for writing can help every child to develop as a reader. With the spread of ability found in many classrooms, it can be a challenge to ensure the lessons meet the needs of every child though.

Guided reading

Skills/Knowledge coverage
- Apply phonic knowledge and skills to read most words quickly and accurately
- Develop comprehension
- Develop reading fluency and stamina
- Develop knowledge about a range of texts, genres and authors
- Participate in discussions about books
- Develop grammar, punctuation, vocabulary and spelling
- Develop reading for pleasure

Notes
Guided Reading is a powerful way of supporting children to make progress in English, teaching both word reading and comprehension using a text that has been carefully selected to provide an appropriate level of challenge.

Guided reading allows for plenty of teacher-child and child-child dialogue, and collaborative learning. In addition, it can provide a regular and supportive time for children to read engaging texts that will resonate with their interests and capture their imagination, giving the children the satisfaction of enjoying a whole book from beginning to end. Over the course of a school year, children will have the chance to explore a wide range of genres, some of which will be new or unfamiliar, but all of which help children broaden their reading experience and form opinions about books and authors. Guided reading also gives children access to the language of books and literature.

If and other poems (Oxford Level 15)

reading provision

Reading 1:1 with an adult

Skills/Knowledge coverage
- Apply phonic knowledge and skills to read most words quickly and accurately
- Develop comprehension
- Develop reading stamina
- Develop knowledge about a range of texts, genres and authors
- Develop reading for pleasure
- Develop grammar, punctuation, vocabulary and spelling

Notes
1:1 reading can be a powerful tool in supporting children to develop as readers. The key, as with all types of reading, is accurate assessment, carefully matched texts, careful planning and quality dialogue. Organizing reading like this depends on having a large number of adults or older children available, and many of the benefits of this approach are also present in small group-work.

Independent reading

Skills/Knowledge coverage
- Apply phonic knowledge and skills to read most words quickly and accurately
- Develop comprehension
- Develop reading stamina
- Develop knowledge about a range of texts, genres and authors
- Develop reading for pleasure
- Can facilitate discussions about books
- Develop grammar, punctuation, vocabulary and spelling

Notes
Independent reading at school is an important way of helping children to develop as self-reliant readers, able to select a book and maintain sustained concentration. Independent reading is an equitable activity; it means that every child, including those who do not read at home, has time to enjoy a book every day.

Independent reading works best if there is also an opportunity for children to talk about the books they are reading.

Listening to an adult reading aloud

Skills/Knowledge coverage
- Develop comprehension
- Develop knowledge about a range of texts, genres and authors
- Participate in discussions about books
- Develop grammar and vocabulary
- Develop reading for pleasure

Notes
Reading aloud to children provides opportunities to listen to a model of fluent reading. Through discussion about the text, children will be able to develop their comprehension skills. It is also an opportunity for children to simply enjoy a story, helping them to develop a love of books and reading.

Reading intervention

Skills/Knowledge coverage
- Develop phonic knowledge and word reading
- Develop comprehension
- Develop reading fluency and stamina
- Develop grammar, punctuation, vocabulary and spelling
- Participate in discussions about books
- Develop reading enjoyment

Notes
Run either 1:1 or in small groups, reading intervention provides opportunities to focus on the skills children need to develop to catch up with their peers. Sessions need to be carefully matched to the needs of each child and ongoing assessments made to ensure children are making rapid progress.

Addressing the core reading and spoken language skills

Research shows there are several important factors in helping children to become successful readers who understand what they read and who enjoy reading. **Project X** *Origins* draws on this research which emphasizes the following factors:

❯ Word reading

Project X *Origins* gives pupils the opportunity to apply their developing knowledge in a real reading context with books that provide an appropriate level of challenge. As children progress and become confident word readers, the **Project X** *Origins graphic texts* continue to provide opportunities to apply decoding skills whenever they encounter new or unfamiliar words, to explore the meaning and origins of unfamiliar words, and to recognize different spelling rules.

❯ Vocabulary

Project X *Origins* includes explicit work on enriching children's vocabulary, equipping them with a large bank of words, which is vital to developing comprehension and fluency. Understanding individual words and their meanings enables children to make sense of what they read, in English and across the wider curriculum. As children progress and develop as word readers, reading is the principal way children encounter new words, further developing their vocabulary.

A vocabulary chart for each book shows when key vocabulary is introduced, identifying challenge and context words for each book (see pages 46–49 for an overview).

❯ Comprehension

Building strong comprehension skills is central to becoming an effective reader. High-quality discussion and focused questioning are two of the most effective ways of developing children's understanding and both are significant aspects of **Project X** *Origins*. The Guided Reading Notes highlight opportunities for teaching specific comprehension skills and provide guidance to support effective questioning. The notes are built to work around the following key comprehension strategies:

- Previewing/predicting
- Activating and building prior knowledge
- Questioning (child to child and child to text)
- Recall
- Visualization and other sensory responses
- Deducing, inferring and drawing conclusions
- Synthesizing
- Summarizing/determining importance
- Empathizing
- Personal responses including adopting a critical stance

⟩⟩ Fluency

Working in a small group with a text matched to children's ability can support children to develop fluency, offering opportunities to listen to books being read and to read aloud themselves. Other children in the group act as both an audience and a model for expressive reading.

⟩⟩ Supporting reading for pleasure

Developing word reading and comprehension form the core of learning to read, but on their own they are not enough to help children to become fluent lifelong readers. To achieve this, children need to be engaged with reading and shown how exciting and joyful books can be. The **Project X Origins** books have been written to do just this – broaden children's reading experience, help them to form opinions about whole books and authors, and give them access to the language of books and literature. Working with a text that has been carefully selected to match their current reading level with an appropriate degree of challenge means children can access the text with confidence whilst at the same time developing their reading skills.

⟩⟩ Spelling, punctuation and grammar

Learning about grammar and punctuation in the context of a text, rather than through a series of discrete exercises, can help to make grammar and punctuation relevant; seeing how real authors use punctuation and grammar for effect in books enables children to see the important role they can play in effective communication. The **Project X Origins** Guided Reading Notes outline opportunities for developing pupils' understanding of these aspects of language for every book in the series (see pages 46–49 for an overview).

The Guided Reading Notes also support the teaching of spelling, identifying key words and activities to teach specific spelling objectives drawn from the English National Curriculum. Considering spelling in the context of guided reading sessions can help to consolidate learning and develop an understanding of the words and their meanings. Working in a small group organized by pupils' needs means that the learning objectives can be matched to children's language development more accurately than when working as a whole class. The use of texts closely matched to the needs of readers also supports this. **Project X** *Origins* provides an ideal forum for pupils to practise using the technical language to describe different punctuation and grammar features, providing opportunities to address any misconceptions as they occur.

Spoken language

Children's oral language and their ability to listen to others are crucial to the development of thinking and communication skills and underpin much of their learning, including learning to read.

The small-group structure of guided reading is an excellent way to support the development of children's spoken language; children have more frequent opportunities to ask and answer questions and to contribute to the discussion. **Project X** *Origins* provides opportunities for children to:

- discuss and debate their ideas with others
- justify their opinions
- ask and answer questions
- develop their vocabulary
- explore and hypothesize
- describe and explain
- listen to and consider the ideas of others.

Great Space Explorers
(Oxford Level 17)

Guided reading progression

Guided reading can play an important role in helping readers at every stage of their reading development – from the very early stages of learning to read right through to when children are independent and able readers.

As children move through the school, developing as readers, guided reading sessions are likely to focus on teaching different aspects of reading. **Project X** *Origins* has been developed to support teachers to tailor their guided reading sessions to the needs of children at different stages of their development, helping every child to become a confident, competent and keen reader both able to decode and understand what they read.

Once children have become secure in their word reading, **Project X** *Origins* continues to provide opportunities to practise and apply these skills as children encounter challenging vocabulary and explore the meaning and origins of unfamiliar words. Opportunities to develop their fluency, through frequent opportunities to read and reread texts, are embedded throughout **Project X** *Origins* and children are supported in developing comprehension strategies that allow them to tackle more challenging texts so that they are not only able to read but also able to understand what they read.

Once children have become confident, independent readers, **Project X** *Origins* continues to support children's reading development, providing opportunities to explore increasingly challenging texts in depth, developing critical thinking skills and applying comprehension strategies to understand more complex narratives and content.

Great Inventors (Oxford Level 15)

The National Curriculum in England

Project X *Origins* has been developed to help schools meet the challenges of the new English curriculum, with finely levelled texts and guided reading activities that support the development of children's language and literacy skills from Reception to Year 6.

Project X *Origins* is fully in line with the aims of the new English curriculum to ensure children develop strong spoken language and reading skills as well as a love of reading, ensuring that children are able to:

- read easily, fluently and with good understanding,
- develop the habit of reading widely and often, for both pleasure and information,
- acquire a wide vocabulary, an understanding of grammar and knowledge of linguistic conventions for reading, writing and spoken language,
- use discussion in order to learn,
- are competent in the arts of speaking and listening.

Project X Origins helps teachers meet the demands of the curriculum in the following ways:

Key features of the National Curriculum for English	Project X *Origins*
Focus on reading for pleasure	- Features characters that will excite 21st-century children - Is designed to appeal to boys, without discouraging girls - Ensures children encounter a range of genres, many of which will be new or unfamiliar - Gives children a regular time to read
Comprehension taught through texts that provide an increasing level of challenge	- Provides comprehensive Guided Reading Notes that highlight opportunities for teaching specific comprehension skills and strategies - Provides guidance to support effective questioning - Includes stimulating fiction, poetry and non-fiction that offers scope to develop children's comprehension skills - Features a structure of finely levelled books that grow progressively more challenging to meet the needs of children at every stage of their reading development
Spoken language and discussion a key part of teaching reading	- Provides Guided Reading Notes that support teachers to run guided reading sessions built on high-quality discussion and focused questioning of children - Provides opportunities for children to share their understanding of books - Includes additional drama and role-play activities to help children adopt and sustain roles, and build their confidence - Provides opportunities for collaborative pair- and group-work

Key features of the National Curriculum for English	Project X *Origins*
Focus on children's accurate use grammar, punctuation and spelling	▪ Outlines specific grammar, punctuation and spelling objectives drawn from the National Curriculum ▪ Features 'developing grammar, punctuation and spelling' sections for every book, highlighting opportunities to teach this element of English in the context of reading
Emphasis on vocabulary development	▪ Features 'developing vocabulary' sections to support teachers to meet this requirement ▪ **Project X *Origins* graphic texts** contextualize archaic and poetic language ▪ Books are written to encompass a wide age-appropriate lexicon, including some technical or specialist language in non-fiction texts

For specific advice on **Project X *Origins* graphic texts** and the curriculum, please refer to page 16.

> **A note on curricula correlation**
>
> Guided reading offers opportunities to cover a large number of reading and oracy objectives. The **Project X *Origins* graphic texts** Guided Reading Notes highlight the most relevant National Curriculum objectives for England for each book. In addition there is also the potential to cover more objectives, depending on the needs of each group, both within the session and through follow-up work.
>
> The very nature of guided reading means that many objectives will be covered every time teachers run a session; objectives such as these have not been repeated for each title but are asterisked on the following charts.
>
> It is sometimes the case that there are objectives that would be more appropriate to address outside of the guided reading sessions such as in whole-class teaching. Other objectives may be better met by using non-graphic texts. When objectives such as these occur, they have not been correlated to the Guided Reading Notes. These are also indicated on the following charts.

The National Curriculum in England
Years 3 and 4 programmes of study

	Grey Book Band/Oxford Level 14			Dark Blue Book Band/Oxford Level 15				
	Chasing Birdy	The Wind in the Willows	The Pelican Chorus and other poems	Great Artists	Time Stealer	The Jungle Book	If and other poems	Great Inventors
Spoken language								
Listen and respond appropriately to adults and their peers *		•						
Ask relevant questions to extend their understanding and knowledge		•					•	•
Use relevant strategies to build their vocabulary	•				•			
Articulate and justify answers, arguments and opinions								
Give well-structured descriptions, explanations and narratives for different purposes, including for expressing feelings			•			•		
Maintain attention and participate actively in collaborative conversations, staying on topic and initiating and responding to comments *								
Use spoken language to develop understanding through speculating, hypothesising, imagining and exploring ideas *								
Speak audibly and fluently with an increasing command of Standard English **								
Participate in discussions, presentations, performances, role play, improvisations and debates *								
Gain, maintain and monitor the interest of the listener(s) *								
Consider and evaluate different viewpoints, attending to and building on the contributions of others				•			•	
Select and use appropriate registers for effective communication **		•		•				
Word reading								
Apply their growing knowledge of root words, prefixes and suffixes (etymology and morphology) as listed in English Appendix 1, both to read aloud and to understand the meaning of new words they meet			•				•	•
Read further exception words, noting the unusual correspondences between spelling and sound, and where these occur in the word	•				•	•		

	Grey Book Band/Oxford Level 14				Dark Blue Book Band/Oxford Level 15			
	Chasing Birdy	The Wind in the Willows	The Pelican Chorus and other poems	Great Artists	Time Stealer	The Jungle Book	If and other poems	Great Inventors
Comprehension								
Develop positive attitudes to reading and understanding of what they read by:								
Listening to and discussing a wide range of fiction, poetry, plays, non-fiction and reference books or textbooks *			•					
Reading books that are structured in different ways and reading for a range of purposes								
Using dictionaries to check the meaning of words that they have read		•			•			
Increasing their familiarity with a wide range of books, including fairy stories, myths and legends, and retelling some of these orally *						•		
Identifying themes and conventions in a wide range of books								
Preparing poems and play scripts to read aloud and to perform, showing understanding through intonation, tone, volume and action			•				•	
Discussing words and phrases that capture the reader's interest and imagination			•				•	
Recognising some different forms of poetry [for example, free verse, narrative poetry]			•				•	
Understand what they read, in books they can read independently, by:								
Checking that the text makes sense to them, discussing their understanding and explaining the meaning of words in context	•			•				
Asking questions to improve their understanding of a text	•			•			•	
Drawing inferences such as inferring characters' feelings, thoughts and motives from their actions, and justifying inferences with evidence	•	•			•	•		
Predicting what might happen from details stated and implied	•	•						
Identifying main ideas drawn from more than one paragraph and summarising these		•			•	•	•	•
Identifying how language, structure, and presentation contribute to meaning		•			•	•	•	•
Retrieve and record information from non-fiction				•				•
Participate in discussion about both books that are read to them and those they can read for themselves, taking turns and listening to what others say **								

* NOTE: This objective will be covered in every guided reading session
** NOTE: This objective is best addressed outside of the guided reading session

The National Curriculum in England
Years 5 and 6 programmes of study

	Dark Blue Book Band/ Oxford Level 16				Dark Red Book Band/ Oxford Level 17				Dark Red Book Band/ Oxford Level 18				Dark Red+ Book Band/ Oxford Level 19				Dark Red+ Book Band/ Oxford Level 20			
	The Sands of Deception	The Secret Garden	I Wandered Lonely as a Cloud and other poems	Great Naturalists	The Jurchen Recruits	Treasure Island	The Pied Piper of Hamelin	Great Space Explorers	Time's Pendulum	Alice's Adventures in Wonderland	Jabberwocky and other poems	Great Scientists	Antarctic Ambush	The Call of the Wild	The Raven and other poems	Great Engineers	Time Runs Out	Oliver Twist	For the Fallen and other poems	Great Pioneers
Spoken language																				
Listen and respond appropriately to adults and their peers *	•																			
Ask relevant questions to extend their understanding and knowledge										•						•				
Use relevant strategies to build their vocabulary		•	•			•	•			•					•			•	•	
Articulate and justify answers, arguments and opinions							•		•						•					
Give well-structured descriptions, explanations and narratives for different purposes, including for expressing feelings				•	•			•			•	•	•				•	•		•
Maintain attention and participate actively in collaborative conversations, staying on topic and initiating and responding to comments *																				
Use spoken language to develop understanding through speculating, hypothesising, imagining and exploring ideas *																				
Speak audibly and fluently with an increasing command of Standard English **																				
Participate in discussions, presentations, performances, role play, improvisations and debates *																				
Gain, maintain and monitor the interest of the listener(s) *																				
Consider and evaluate different viewpoints, attending to and building on the contributions of others		•												•						
Select and use appropriate registers for effective communication **																				

42

		Dark Blue Book Band / Oxford Level 16				Dark Red Book Band / Oxford Level 17				Dark Red Book Band / Oxford Level 18				Dark Red+ Book Band / Oxford Level 19				Dark Red+ Book Band / Oxford Level 20			
		The Sands of Deception	The Secret Garden	I Wandered Lonely as a Cloud and other poems	Great Naturalists	The Jurchen Recruits	Treasure Island	The Pied Piper of Hamelin	Great Space Explorers	Time's Pendulum	Alice's Adventures in Wonderland	Jabberwocky and other poems	Great Scientists	Antarctic Ambush	The Call of the Wild	The Raven and other poems	Great Engineers	Time Runs Out	Oliver Twist	For the Fallen and other poems	Great Pioneers
Word reading	Apply their growing knowledge of root words, prefixes and suffixes (etymology and morphology) as listed in English Appendix 1, both to read aloud and to understand the meaning of new words they meet	•	•	•	•	•	•	•	•	•	•	•	•	•	•	•	•	•	•	•	•
Comprehension	Maintain positive attitudes to reading and understanding of what they read by:																				
	Continuing to read and discuss an increasingly wide range of fiction, poetry, plays, non-fiction and reference books or textbooks *			•																	
	Reading books that are structured in different ways and reading for a range of purposes				•							•					•				•
	Increasing their familiarity with a wide range of books, including myths, legends, and traditional stories, modern fiction, fiction from our literary heritage, and books from other cultures and traditions		•			•	•				•				•				•		
	Recommending books that they have read to their peers, giving reasons for their choices **															•				•	
	Identifying and discussing themes and conventions in and across a wide range of writing							•							•						
	Making comparisons within and across books			•							•		•								
	Learning a wider range of poetry by heart											•									
	Preparing poems and plays to read aloud and to perform, showing understanding through intonation, tone and volume so that the meaning is clear to an audience											•				•				•	

* NOTE: This objective will be covered in every guided reading session
** NOTE: This objective is best addressed outside of the guided reading session

43

The National Curriculum in England
Years 5 and 6 programmes of study

	Dark Blue Book Band/ Oxford Level 16				Dark Red Book Band/ Oxford Level 17				Dark Red Book Band/ Oxford Level 18				Dark Red+ Book Band/ Oxford Level 19				Dark Red+ Book Band/ Oxford Level 20			
	The Sands of Deception	The Secret Garden	I Wandered Lonely as a Cloud and other poems	Great Naturalists	The Jurchen Recruits	Treasure Island	The Pied Piper of Hamelin	Great Space Explorers	Time's Pendulum	Alice's Adventures in Wonderland	Jabberwocky and other poems	Great Scientists	Antarctic Ambush	The Call of the Wild	The Raven and other poems	Great Engineers	Time Runs Out	Oliver Twist	For the Fallen and other poems	Great Pioneers
Understand what they read by:																				
Checking that the book makes sense to them, discussing their understanding and exploring the meaning of words in context	•	•					•													
Asking questions to improve their understanding				•					•	•										
Drawing inferences such as inferring characters' feelings, thoughts and motives from their actions, and justifying inferences with evidence	•	•			•	•			•	•				•				•		
Predicting what might happen from details stated and implied	•								•								•			
Summarising the main ideas drawn from more than one paragraph, identifying key details that support the main ideas				•		•		•				•		•						
Identifying how language, structure and presentation contribute to meaning			•				•				•		•	•	•	•	•	•	•	•
Discuss and evaluate how authors use language, including figurative language, considering the impact on the reader			•				•				•				•				•	
Distinguish between statements of fact and opinion												•								•
Retrieve, record and present information from non-fiction				•								•				•				
Participate in discussions about books that are read to them and those they can read for themselves, building on their own and others' ideas and challenging views courteously *																				
Explain and discuss their understanding of what they have read, including through formal presentations and debates, maintaining a focus on the topic and using notes where necessary *													•							
Provide reasoned justifications for their views								•	•							•	•	•		•

* NOTE: This objective will be covered in every guided reading session
** NOTE: This objective is best addressed outside of the guided reading session

The National Curriculum in England
Spelling, vocabulary, punctuation and grammar coverage (Year 4)

	Title	Spelling	Vocabulary (challenge and context words)	Punctuation	Grammar
Grey Book Band / Oxford Level 14	Chasing Birdy	Words with the /k/ sound and words with the /sh/ sound spelt 'ch'	concentrate, overdue, cautiously, walkway, intense, vortex, activated, mode, technology, precise, visual, accomplished, adjustments, experience, locate, effective, cartridges, exposed, prototype, destination, artefacts, devastating anatomy, mysterious		Noun phrases expanded by the addition of modifying adjectives, nouns and preposition phrases
	The Wind in the Willows	The suffix -ous	highwaymen, scoundrels, wrecked, punishment, harsh, seize, familiar, outrageous, passage, pantry, bloodthirsty, ruthless, murderous, panicked, contentment, courage, banquet, opportunity, modest, inspiration		Appropriate choice of **pronoun** or **noun** within and across **sentences** to aid **cohesion** and avoid repetition
	The Pelican Chorus and other poems	Homophones and near-homophones	leathery, flumpy, ought, received, wondrous, multitude, delicate, violent, waddling, form, wreath, vowed, lengthening, twilight, lessening, dwells, gingham, calico, spat, wallowed, employing, exaggerate, torrents, encouraging, saluted, ingenious, inspiration, notion, arrant	Use of inverted commas and other **punctuation** to indicate direct speech	
	Great Artists	Endings which sound like /shun/	rural, fossil, cavern, landscape, inspired, curiosity, perfectionist, erosion, caricature, impression, impressionism, tuberculosis, encouraged, tragedy, masterpiece, expressed, exhibition, expressionism, dyslexic, cubism, surveyor, forms	Use of commas after **fronted adverbials**	**Fronted adverbials**
Dark Blue Book Band / Oxford Level 15	Time Stealer	Homophones and near-homophones	disorientated, artefacts, summit, encamped, chieftains, puny, directive, precise, obscure, stealth, formidable, foe, Achilles heel, humanoid, charred, scout, skirting, oblivious, seize, region, vulnerable		The grammatical difference between **plural** and **possessive** -s
	The Jungle Book	Words with endings sounding like /chuh/	scrounging, mischief, quarry, fostering, Council, inspect, admired, deceitful, lawless, singed, adapted, content, ravine, cast out, sequel	Use of commas after **fronted adverbials**	**Fronted adverbials**
	If and other poems	The suffix -ly	allowances, triumph, imposters, knaves, stoop, pitch-and-toss, sinew, virtue, foes, unforgiving, ore-bed, furnace, wrought, tooled, gauged, thousandth, monstrous, quay, barren, wilderness, aloft, cisterns, irrigate, dammed, coppice, heath, anemones, broods, cantering, solitudes, rime	**Apostrophes** to mark **plural** possession	
	Great Inventors	The prefixes in- and im-	pi, radius, irrigate, summon, volume, irregular, siege, reflective, accessible, revolt, fascinated, de-husking, automaton, telegraph, patent office, campaigner, hydrofoil, conduct, phonograph, filament, carbonized, facility, cylinder, apparatus, prejudice, officials, citizens		Appropriate choice of **pronoun** or **noun** within and across **sentences** to aid **cohesion** and avoid repetition

The National Curriculum in England
Spelling, vocabulary, punctuation and grammar coverage (Year 5)

	Title	Spelling	Vocabulary (challenge and context words)	Punctuation	Grammar
Dark Blue Book Band / Oxford Level 16	The Sands of Deception	Words ending in -able and -ible	sundial, ancestors, particles, apparel, evade, procession, precariously, ventilation, colossal, somersaults, impersonated, immobilize, radically, altered, premises, forbidding, commencing, paralysis, space-time continuum, enveloped, duration, adjusted, archaeologists, revered	Brackets, dashes or commas to indicate parenthesis	
	The Secret Garden	Words containing the letter-string ough	confine, lass, moor, rugged, tamed, intrigued, trepidation, orchard, mite, eluded, wuthering, weathered, steeled, compelled, exquisite, amuse, sow, monsoon, pacified, tranquil, spirits, overwhelmed, blossomed, depicting, erected		Indicating degrees of possibility using **adverbs** [for example, *perhaps, surely*] or **modal verbs** [for example, *might, should, will, must*]
	I Wandered Lonely as a Cloud *and other poems*	Homophones and other words that are often confused	vales, host, continuous, margin, bay, sprightly, glee, jocund, wealth, oft, pensive, inward, bliss, solitude, picturesque, meadow, abroad, lea, wary, hi, squadron, wicket, brine, vast, lichens, turf, gluten, aliment, sluggish, suspended, disporting, flukes, leaden-eyed, pursuits, thence, subtle, sphere, siblings, thee, spray, mount, infinity, governess, initially	Brackets, dashes or commas to indicate parenthesis	
	Great Naturalists	Words with 'silent' letters	species, evolved, argumentative, conservation, habitats, rumoured, settlers, expeditions, pollinate, nectar, antennae, honeycomb, waggle, physiology, zoology, institute, palaeontologist, landslide, fossilized, extinct, Geological Society, spores, memorial, dedicated, fellow, biodiversity, generations		**Relative clauses** beginning with *who, which, where, when, whose, that,* or an omitted relative pronoun
	The Jurchen Recruits	Endings which sound like /chul/	braced, mechanical, chain drive, dismantled, approximately, inspired, reckless, novices, recruits, slack off, unaware, commence, wary, armillary sphere, longitude, latitude, mannequins, relentless, sturdy, paralysis dismantled, dejected, components, prototype, celestial, hydraulics		**Verb prefix** re–
Dark Red Book Band / Oxford Level 17	Treasure Island	Words with endings sounding like /sure/ or /ture/*	secretive, insisted, summons, squire, legendary, expedition, mutiny, aye, galley, ration, rogues, ahoy, stockade, mutineers, evaded, marooned, retreated, diversion, adrift, unconscious, currents, truce, convoke, council, deposed, elect, double-cross, scoundrel, beached, negotiate, cheaply, ample	Use of commas to clarify meaning or avoid ambiguity	
	The Pied Piper of Hamelin	The suffix -ly *	ditty, kegs, sprats, noddy, Corporation, ermine, dolts, rouse, remedy, quaked, consternation, guilder, swarthy, quaint, attire, gnats, adept, uttered, brawny, tawny, plunged, quoth, thrifty, trifling, pottage, Caliph, bate a stiver, brook, fowls, flaxen, rack, wretched, lo, wondrous, portal, bereft, hue, endeavour, decree, duly, tabor, hostelry, mirth, solemn, ascribe, outlandish, subterraneous, trepanned, scores, aught		**Relative clauses** beginning with *who, which, where, when, whose, that,* or an omitted relative pronoun
	Great Space Explorers	Words containing the letter-string ough	astronomer, observations, unwavering, compile, catalogues, eclipse, stationary, lunar, solar, astrolabe, quadrant, sphere, persuaded, outrage, unquenchable, supernova, lens, ingenious, handsomely, nocturnal, decades, fortunate, observatory, efficiently, analyse, stellar spectra, opportunity, mere, nova(e), nebula(e), magnitude, expanding, orbited, probes, module, microgravity		Indicating degrees of possibility using **adverbs** [for example, *perhaps, surely*] or **modal verbs** [for example, *might, should, will, must*]

* NOTE: This focus is taken from the Year 3–4 spelling list but is included here as a useful practice point

The National Curriculum in England
Spelling, vocabulary, punctuation and grammar coverage (Year 6)

	Title	Spelling	Vocabulary (challenge and context words)	Punctuation	Grammar
Dark Red Book Band / Oxford Level 18	Time's Pendulum	Words with the 'ei' sound spelt ei, eigh, or ey *	attic, blaze, pendulum, emerged, rickety, eased, remarkable, loomed, exposed, hesitated, manner, shattering, colony, extraordinary, species, breakthrough, jest, commence, beseech, hallucinating, acquired, existence, harness, insubstantial, oblivion, enhanced, functionality, roost, cue, good riddance, chime, statesman, formulating, mechanical	Use of the semi-colon, colon and dash to mark boundaries between independent **clauses**	
	Alice's Adventures in Wonderland	Words ending in -ant and -ent	waistcoat, latitude, longitude, curious, ought, bedraggled, Caucus, thimble, disapproving, wretched, serpent, footman, croquet, Duchess, procession, apoplectic, cowering, pardoned, Gryphon, ambition, distraction, uglification, derision, Quadrille, somersault, Knave, verdict, accomplished		How words are related by meaning as synonyms and antonyms
	Jabberwocky and other poems	Words containing the letter-string ough	shun, foe, sought, burbled, slain, chortled, doth, billows, beseech, briny, eager, conveniently, sealing wax, dismal, sympathize, scarcely, recitation, obey, deed, accomplished **		Use of the **passive** to affect the presentation of information in a **sentence**
	Great Scientists	Endings which sound like /shul/	virtual reality, holographic, theory, weary, prism, corrupts, authorities, Universal Gravitation, institution, economy, summoned, fascinated, embarked, gruelling, compile, ponder, generator, authorities, pitchblende, polonium, radium, luminous, radioactivity, recognition, cancerous, patent, persevered, Special Relativity, equations, atomic bomb, influential, photoelectric, pneumonia, excruciating, antiseptic, strategic, crucial, formidable, convoy, laborious, Bombe, decryption, artificial intelligence, binary	**Punctuation** of bullet points to list information	
Dark Red+ Book Band / Oxford Level 19	Antarctic Ambush	Words ending in -able and -ible	parameter, ozone, haywire, pinched, navigate, incredibly, floes, paranoid, lousy, scurvy, presence, baffled, commotion, evaporated, tomfoolery, brig, squabbling, consumed, hull, slamming, starboard, prow, soul, vessels, catastrophic, Geronimo, mere, allies, obtain, resonated, malfunctions, undertook, degrees, confrontation		The difference between structures typical of informal speech and structures appropriate for formal speech and writing
	The Call of the Wild	Homophones and other words that are often confused	veranda, escort, twilight, debt, bargain, viley, companions, approached, throbbed, tireless, propeller, stern, obedience, dispatches, invaluable, loathed, recuperation, inspirational, vast, yabbering, mangy, towed, obliged, dwindled, physically, incapable, guaranteed, arduous, musing, tirelessly, irresistible, impulses, wilderness, insistent, lope, mourned, savage, legendary, prospectors	Linking ideas across paragraphs using a wider range of **cohesive devices:** ellipsis	
	The Raven and other poems	Words ending with the /g/ sound spelt -gue and the /k/ sound spelt -que (French in origin) *	lore, ember, wrought, surcease, entreating, implore, scarce, mortal, lattice, yore, obeisance, mien, beguiling, decorum, countenance, craven, Plutonian, quoth, discourse, placid, unmerciful, dirges, melancholy, gaunt, divining, gloated, censer, respite, nepenthe, quaff, desolate, undaunted, implore, pallid, aspire, sinews, anvil, fissure, slackness, mused, perversity, humility, convulsed, undignified, paltry, vulgar, accursed, exile, expiate, pettiness, azure, imminent, betides, chattels	How hyphens can be used to avoid ambiguity	
	Great Engineers	Endings which sound like /shus/ spelt -cious or -tious	summon, sarcophagus, mastaba, assembled, infected, scribes, feat, amphitheatres, aqueducts, conquer, territories, pontoon, forum, intricate, friezes, banished, ambitious, tirelessly, gorge, fraught, daredevil, viaducts, excavate, maiden voyage, accomplishments, qualifications, caisson, completion, succumb, disbarred, manufacturer, cosmonaut, aeronautical, artificial, alternating current		The difference between vocabulary typical of informal speech and vocabulary appropriate for formal speech and writing

	Title	Spelling	Vocabulary (challenge and context words)	Punctuation	Grammar
Dark Red+ Book Band/ Oxford Level 20	Time Runs Out	Words ending in -ant and -ent	plummeting, collision, deflect, bureau, immobilized, strategy, Geronimo, furtively, execute, formation, complying, malfunction, configure, surveyed, narcissist, impede, salvation, strategic, unimpeded, cybernetics, alleged, sophisticated, descended, footage, nifty, manoeuvres, meddling, annihilate, Caesar, tampered, Cretaceous, desolate, intimidated, synchronize, megalomaniac, despot, redemption, unconscious, sacrificed, resign, materializes, calibrated, diversified, frequency		The difference between vocabulary typical of informal speech and vocabulary appropriate for formal speech and writing
	Oliver Twist	Homophones and other words that are often confused	Parish, Beadle, pauper, idling, oakum, gruel, apprentice, authority, disposed, burden, millstone, victuals, Workie, liberal, vastness, lodgings, Magistrates' Court, vagabond, worship, scoundrel, shamming, traps, mite, wretch, plate, blabbed, discreet, skulk, noose, constables		Use of the **passive** to affect the presentation of information in a **sentence**
	For the Fallen and other poems	Words with the 'i' sound spelt ei after c	thanksgiving, solemn, august, desolation, staunch, profound, Five-Nines, ecstacy, flound'ring, guttering, smothering, writhing, froth-corrupted, obscene, incurable, ardent, bade, tumult, conquest, gropers, tapering, Sabbath, ascending, phantom, full-key'd, convulsive, foremost, assault, veterans, enwraps, up-buoying, twain, adjutant, league, blunder'd, volley'd, sabres, plunged, reel'd, sunder'd		Layout devices
	Great Pioneers	Words with 'silent' letters	trailblazers, tenacious, applicants, exhibition, transmits, bulletin, analogue, striving, suffragettes, obstruction, radical, horizon, navigation, altimeter, transatlantic, commemorative, turbojet, outbreak, allies, biplanes, ditched, emigrated, phonograph, wilderness, patents, atmosphere, bathyscaphe, expeditions, apartheid, overthrow, sentenced, negotiation, Republic, honorary, aviators, legacy, deforestation	**Punctuation** of bullet points to list information	

* NOTE: This focus is taken from the Year 3–4 spelling list but is included here as a useful practice point
** NOTE: Jabberwocky contains a large number of nonsense words, such as 'brillig' and 'slithy' which will also present a challenge to the reader. These have not been listed here.

Links to the Scottish Curriculum for Excellence

Project X *Origins* has been developed to reflect and support the purposes and principles of the Curriculum for Excellence (CfE). Motivating, finely levelled texts and guided reading activities support the development of literacy and English skills from Primary 5 to Primary 7.

Reading engagement

The CfE recognizes the findings of research, indicating that there is a significant link between reading success, the enjoyment of books, and the number of books that children read. Reading experiences and outcomes embody the principles of choice, enjoyment, personal preference and interest. The CfE demands that young readers interrogate, discuss and formulate their own questions about the texts they read. **Project X** *Origins* provides children with a diverse and motivating range of books and the Guided Reading Notes teach them how to engage in constructive dialogue about these texts.

Developing critical thinking and text analysis

Each set of Guided Reading Notes is fully correlated to outcomes for the CfE and provides a model for running effective guided reading sessions, including opportunities to focus on:

- **Listening and talking:** Project X *Origins* Guided Reading Notes place a strong emphasis on the importance of listening and talking both as a precursor to successful reading, comprehension and writing and as a means of ensuring that children become confident individuals and effective contributors. Children are encouraged to talk before, during and after reading, to express preferences and to give and justify their opinions about a book. In addition, there are opportunities for collaborative pair- and group-work, for giving presentations and for drama activities.

- **Reading:** Project X *Origins* Guided Reading Notes provide explicit opportunities for the development of comprehension strategies before, during and after reading, ensuring children are engaged in using tools for reading; finding and using information; and analyzing, evaluating and understanding texts.

- **Writing:** also included in the Guided Reading Notes are a range of follow-up activities to support the link from reading into writing, using the knowledge children have developed through in-depth exploration of the text and applying to their own writing.

Literacy across the curriculum

The CfE strongly recommends that reading is taught in every subject area. This principle ensures that children learn the difference in structure, vocabulary and style of science, historical or drama texts, for example. This approach makes the teaching of reading coherent.

Through its inclusion of cross-curricular activities and links to other subject areas, **Project X Origins** encourages children to develop and apply literacy skills across other curriculum subjects and to become successful learners. The Guided Reading Notes provide a range of follow-up activities, many of which are active and hands-on, to support the practical application of literacy skills in a range of contexts. Further ideas for taking this approach to learning are given on page 70 of this handbook.

Assessment

Formative assessment drives learning in Scottish education. In reading, this involves teachers in evaluating their pupils' understanding and deciding next steps based on the questioning and observation of their pupils as they work. This process of responding and targeting children's changing needs will be greatly assisted by the assessment prompts built in to the Guided Reading Notes for every **Project X Origins** book. These assessment criteria, drawn from the Oxford Reading Criterion Scale, are graded in a coherent progression of skill and correlate appropriately with the CfE. For more information on the Oxford Reading Criterion Scale, please see page 83.

> **A note on curricular correlation**
>
> Guided reading offers opportunities to cover a large number of reading and oracy objectives. The **Project X Origins graphic texts** Guided Reading Notes highlight the most relevant objectives from the Scottish Curriculum for Excellence for each book.
>
> The very nature of guided reading means that many objectives will be covered every time teachers run a session; objectives such as these have not been repeated for each title but are asterisked on the following charts.
>
> It is sometimes the case that there are objectives that would be more appropriate to address outside of the guided reading sessions such as in whole-class teaching. Other objectives may be better met by using non-graphic texts. When objectives such as these occur, they have not been correlated to the Guided Reading Notes. These are also indicated on the following charts.

Scottish Curriculum for Excellence
Literacy and English experiences and outcomes (Primary 5–Primary 6)

	Grey Book Band/ Oxford Level 14				Dark Blue Book Band/ Oxford Level 15				Dark Blue Book Band/ Oxford Level 16				Dark Red Book Band/ Oxford Level 17			
	Chasing Birdy	The Wind in the Willows	The Pelican Chorus and other poems	Great Artists	Time Stealer	The Jungle Book	*If* and other poems	Great Inventors	The Sands of Deception	The Secret Garden	*I Wandered Lonely as a Cloud* and other poems	Great Naturalists	The Jurchen Recruits	Treasure Island	The Pied Piper of Hamelin	Great Space Explorers
Listening and talking																
I regularly select and listen to or watch texts which I enjoy and find interesting, and I can explain why I prefer certain sources LIT 1-01a/LIT 2-01a **																
When I engage with others, I can respond in ways appropriate to my role, show that I value others' contributions and use these to build on thinking LIT 2-02a				•		•				•						
I can recognise how the features of spoken language can help in communication, and I can use what I learn ENG 2-03a			•		•											
I can select ideas and relevant information, organise these in an appropriate way for my purpose and use suitable vocabulary for my audience LIT 2-06a		•										•	•			•
I can show my understanding of what I listen to or watch by responding to literal, inferential, evaluative and other types of questions, and by asking different kinds of questions of my own LIT 2-07a									•						•	
To help me develop an informed view, I can distinguish fact from opinion, and I am learning to recognise when my sources try to influence me and how useful these are LIT 2-08a								•			•					
When listening and talking with others for different purposes, I can share information, experiences and opinions LIT 2-09a	•						•							•		

52

	Grey Book Band/ Oxford Level 14				Dark Blue Book Band/ Oxford Level 15				Dark Blue Book Band/ Oxford Level 16				Dark Red Book Band/ Oxford Level 17			
	Chasing Birdy	The Wind in the Willows	The Pelican Chorus and other poems	Great Artists	Time Stealer	The Jungle Book	It and other poems	Great Inventors	The Sands of Deception	The Secret Garden	I Wandered Lonely as a Cloud and other poems	Great Naturalists	The Jurchen Recruits	Treasure Island	The Pied Piper of Hamelin	Great Space Explorers
I regularly select and read, listen to or watch texts which I enjoy and find interesting, and I can explain why I prefer certain texts and authors LIT 1-11a / LIT 2-11a	•		•			•				•						
Through developing my knowledge of context clues, punctuation, grammar and layout, I can read unfamiliar texts with increasing fluency, understanding and expression. ENG 2-12a / ENG 3-12a / ENG 4-12a		•					•				•				•	
I can select and use a range of strategies and resources before I read, and as I read, to make meaning clear and give reasons for my selection LIT 2-13a	•	•		•			•			•				•		
Using what I know about the features of different types of texts, I can find, select and sort information from a variety of sources and use this for different purposes LIT 2-14a							•	•								•
I can make notes, organise them under suitable headings and use them to understand information, develop my thinking, explore problems and create new texts, using my own words as appropriate. LIT 2-15a **																
To show my understanding across different areas of learning, I can identify and consider the purpose and main ideas of a text and use supporting detail LIT 2-16a	•			•	•	•		•	•	•	•	•	•		•	
To show my understanding, I can respond to literal, inferential and evaluative questions and other close reading tasks and can create different kinds of questions of my own ENG 2-17a		•			•	•			•	•	•	•	•	•	•	
To help me develop an informed view, I can distinguish fact from opinion, and I am learning to recognise when my sources try to influence me and how useful these are LIT 2-18a								•				•				
I can: • discuss structure, characterisation and/or setting • recognise the relevance of the writer's theme and how this relates to my own and others' experiences • discuss the writer's style and other features appropriate to genre ENG 2-19a		•	•		•				•		•		•	•		

Reading

* NOTE: This objective will be covered in every guided reading session
** NOTE: This objective is best addressed outside of the guided reading session

Scottish Curriculum for Excellence
Literacy and English experiences and outcomes (Primary 7)

	Dark Red Book Band / Oxford Level 18				Dark Red+ Book Band / Oxford Level 19				Dark Red+ Book Band / Oxford Level 20			
	Time's Pendulum	Alice's Adventures in Wonderland	Jabberwocky and other poems	Great Scientists	Antarctic Ambush	The Call of the Wild	The Raven and other poems	Great Engineers	Time Runs Out	Oliver Twist	For the Fallen and other poems	Great Pioneers
Listening and talking												
I regularly select and listen to or watch texts which I enjoy and find interesting, and I can explain why I prefer certain sources LIT 1-01a/LIT 2-01a **												
When I engage with others, I can respond in ways appropriate to my role, show that I value others' contributions and use these to build on thinking LIT 2-02a			•					•	•	•		
I can recognise how the features of spoken language can help in communication, and I can use what I learn ENG 2-03a	•											
I can select ideas and relevant information, organise these in an appropriate way for my purpose and use suitable vocabulary for my audience LIT 2-06a							•				•	
I can show my understanding of what I listen to or watch by responding to literal, inferential, evaluative and other types of questions, and by asking different kinds of questions of my own LIT 2-07a		•				•						
To help me develop an informed view, I am learning to recognise when my sources try to influence me and how useful these are LIT 2-08a				•								•
When listening and talking with others for different purposes, I can share information, experiences and opinions LIT 2-09a					•							

	Dark Red Book Band / Oxford Level 18				Dark Red+ Book Band / Oxford Level 19				Dark Red+ Book Band / Oxford Level 20			
	Time's Pendulum	Alice's Adventures in Wonderland	Jabberwocky and other poems	Great Scientists	Antarctic Ambush	The Call of the Wild	The Raven and other poems	Great Engineers	Time Runs Out	Oliver Twist	For the Fallen and other poems	Great Pioneers
Reading												
I regularly select and read, listen to or watch texts which I enjoy and find interesting, and I can explain why I prefer certain texts and authors LIT 1-11a / LIT 2-11a		•					•					
Through developing my knowledge of context clues, punctuation, grammar and layout, I can read unfamiliar texts with increasing fluency, understanding and expression ENG 2-12a / ENG 3-12a / ENG 4-12a		•					•					•
I can select and use a range of strategies and resources before I read, and as I read, to make meaning clear and give reasons for my selection LIT 2-13a	•				•							
Using what I know about the features of different types of texts, I can find, select and sort information from a variety of sources and use this for different purposes LIT 2-14a			•	•		•	•	•				
I can make notes, organise them under suitable headings and use them to understand information, develop my thinking, explore problems and create new texts, using my own words as appropriate LIT 2-15a **												
To show my understanding across different areas of learning, I can identify and consider the purpose and main ideas of a text and use supporting detail LIT 2-16a	•	•		•	•				•			
To show my understanding, I can respond to literal, inferential and evaluative questions and other close reading tasks and can create different kinds of questions of my own ENG 2-17a			•			•			•	•		•
To help me develop an informed view, I can identify and explain the difference between fact and opinion, recognise when I am being influenced, and have assessed how useful and believable my sources are LIT 2-18a				•				•			•	
I can: • discuss structure, characterisation and/or setting • recognise the relevance of the writer's theme and how this relates to my own and others' experiences • discuss the writer's style and other features appropriate to genre ENG 2-19a	•		•			•				•	•	

* NOTE: This objective will be covered in every guided reading session
** NOTE: This objective is best addressed outside of the guided reading session

Links to the Programme of Study for English in Wales

Project X *Origins* has been developed in line with the Programme of Study for English in Wales and supports the core literacy aims for Year 4 to Year 6 in the following ways:

Strand 1: Oracy

The Programme of Study stresses the importance of developing oracy and the **Project X** *Origins* Guided Reading Notes provide opportunities to practise and develop speaking, listening, collaboration and discussion. The **Project X** *Origins* books have been designed to stimulate talk and role play, providing plenty of opportunities to explore characters, retell stories, raise and respond to questions, and express opinions. The Guided Reading Notes provide a wealth of opportunities for using talk both as a precursor to successful reading and comprehension, and as a means of ensuring that children become confident individuals and effective contributors. In addition, the follow-up activities offer ideas for pair- and group-work and for drama activities.

Strand 2: Reading

Project X *Origins* supports the two strands highlighted in the Programme of Study: locating, selecting and using information, and responding to what has been read. The **Project X** *Origins* Guided Reading Notes provide opportunities to develop:

- reading strategies
- comprehension
- response and analysis.

Project X *Origins* encourages children to engage in conversations about books, allowing the group/individual to explore the deeper meaning of the text.

Strand 3: Writing

Project X *Origins* includes writing opportunities as part of the follow-up activities for every book, encouraging children to apply the knowledge they have developed through in-depth exploration of the text to their own writing. Photocopiable masters for every book also provide extension activities, including writing opportunities.

The curriculum connection

One of the aims of the Programme of Study for English in Wales is to 'encourage learners to develop and demonstrate their skills in oracy (speaking and listening), reading, and writing for different purposes across the curriculum'.

Through the inclusion of cross-curricular activities and links to other subject areas, **Project X** *Origins* encourages children to develop and apply literacy skills across other curriculum subjects and to become successful learners. The Guided Reading Notes provide a range of follow-up activities, many of which are active and hands-on, to support the practical application of literacy skills in a range of contexts. Further ideas for taking this approach to learning are given on page 70 of this handbook.

Progression and assessment

The Programme of Study recognizes that not all children progress in the same way and at the same pace. **Project X** *Origins* matches the year-by-year breakdown of the Programme of Study, ensuring children have the opportunity to develop the skills they need to progress. The finely levelled **Project X** *Origins* books ensure children can develop the skills they need to progress and build their reading stamina and fluency.

As with the Programme of Study and National tests, **Project X** *Origins* supports both summative and formative assessment helping teachers to build a clear picture of every child's skills and the areas they need to develop – ensuring every child acquires the skills they need to be confident and skilled independent readers. For more information on the Oxford Reading Criterion Scale, please see page 83.

> **A note on curricular correlation**
>
> Guided reading offers opportunities to cover a large number of reading and oracy objectives. The **Project X** *Origins graphic texts* Guided Reading Notes highlight the most relevant objectives from the Programme of Study for English in Wales for each book.
>
> The very nature of guided reading means that many objectives will be covered every time teachers run a session; objectives such as these have not been repeated for each title but are asterisked on the following charts.
>
> It is sometimes the case that there are objectives that would be more appropriate to address outside of the guided reading sessions such as in whole-class teaching. Other objectives may be better met by using non-graphic texts. When objectives such as these occur, they have not been correlated to the Guided Reading Notes. These are also indicated on the following charts.

Programme of Study for English in Wales
Oracy and Reading Key Stage 2 (Year 4)

		Grey Book Band/Oxford Level 14				Dark Blue Book Band/Oxford Level 15			
		Chasing Birdy	The Wind in the Willows	The Pelican Chorus and other poems	Great Artists	Time Stealer	The Jungle Book	If and other poems	Great Inventors
Speaking	Explain information and ideas using supportive resources, e.g. on-screen and web-based materials	•				•			•
	Organise talk so that different audiences can follow what is being said, e.g. giving background information, providing a brief summary of main points			•					
	Explore different situations through role play **								
Listening	Listen carefully to presentations and show understanding of main points **								
	After listening, respond, giving views on what the speaker has said		•						
Collaboration and discussion	Contribute to group discussion and help everyone take part				•		•	•	
	Help a group to reach agreement, e.g. considering reasons or consequences, keeping focus on the topic **	•							
Reading strategies	Use a range of strategies to make meaning from words and sentences, including knowledge of phonics, word roots, word families, syntax, text organisation and prior knowledge of context								
	Read texts, including those with few visual clues, independently with concentration		•			•			
	Use understanding of sentence structure and punctuation to make meaning								
	Skim to gain the gist of a text or the main idea in a chapter				•			•	
	Scan for specific information using a variety of features in texts, e.g. titles, illustrations, key words			•			•		•
	Identify how texts differ in purpose, structure and layout							•	

	Grey Book Band/Oxford Level 14				Dark Blue Book Band/Oxford Level 15			
	Chasing Birdy	The Wind in the Willows	The Pelican Chorus and other poems	Great Artists	Time Stealer	The Jungle Book	If and other poems	Great Inventors
Comprehension								
Accurately identify the main points and supporting information in texts		•	•	•				•
Deduce connections between information, e.g. sequence, importance	•	•			•	•		
Explore information and ideas beyond their personal experience	•		•		•	•		
Response and analysis								
Select and use information and ideas from texts				•				•
Understand how something can be represented in different ways, e.g. moving image, multi-modal and print							•	

* NOTE: This objective will be covered in every guided reading session
** NOTE: This objective is best addressed outside of the guided reading session

Programme of Study for English in Wales
Oracy and Reading Key Stage 2 (Year 5)

		Dark Blue Book Band/Oxford Level 16				Dark Red Book Band/Oxford Level 17			
		The Sands of Deception	The Secret Garden	I Wandered Lonely as a Cloud and other poems	Great Naturalists	The Jurchen Recruits	Treasure Island	The Pied Piper of Hamelin	Great Space Explorers
Speaking	Explain information and ideas, exploring and using ways to be convincing, e.g. *use of vocabulary, gesture, visual aids*	•			•			•	•
	Speak clearly, using formal language and projecting voice effectively to a large audience, e.g. *event for parents/carers, presentation to visitors* **	•							
	Explore issues and themes through role play **								
Listening	Listen carefully to presentations using techniques to remember the main points, e.g. *making notes, summarising* **			•					
	Listen to others, asking questions and responding to both the content and the speakers' viewpoints						•		
Collaboration and discussion	Contribute to group discussion, taking some responsibility for completing the task well, e.g. *introducing relevant ideas, summing up*		•			•			
	Build on and develop the ideas of others in group discussions, e.g. *by asking questions to explore further, offering more ideas*	•				•	•		
Reading strategies	Use a range of strategies to make meaning from words and sentences, including knowledge of phonics, word roots, word families, syntax, text organisation and prior knowledge of context								
	Read extended texts independently for sustained periods *							•	•
	Identify how punctuation relates to sentence structure and how meaning is constructed in complex sentences			•					
	Use a range of strategies for skimming, e.g. *finding key words, phrases, gist, main ideas, themes*		•						
	Scan to find specific details using graphic and textual organisers, e.g. *sub-headings, diagrams*				•				
	Identify features of texts, e.g. *introduction to topic, sequence, illustrations, degree of formality*								•

	Dark Blue Book Band/Oxford Level 16				Dark Red Book Band/Oxford Level 17			
	The Sands of Deception	The Secret Garden	I Wandered Lonely as a Cloud and other poems	Great Naturalists	The Jurchen Recruits	Treasure Island	The Pied Piper of Hamelin	Great Space Explorers
Comprehension								
Show understanding of main ideas and significant details in texts, e.g. mindmapping showing hierarchy of ideas, flowchart identifying a process	•						•	
Infer meaning which is not explicitly stated, e.g. *What happens next?*, *Why did he/she do that?*	•	•	•		•	•	•	
Identify and explore ideas and information that interest them				•	•			•
Gather and organise information and ideas from different sources		•	•	•				
Response and analysis								
Identify what the writer thinks about the topic, e.g. *admires a historical figure, only interested in facts*								
Consider if the content is reliable, e.g. *Are photographs more reliable than drawings?*						•		

* NOTE: This objective will be covered in every guided reading session
** NOTE: This objective is best addressed outside of the guided reading session

Programme of Study for English in Wales
Oracy and Reading Key Stage 2 (Year 6)

		Dark Red Book Band / Oxford Level 18				Dark Red+ Book Band / Oxford Level 19				Dark Red+ Book Band / Oxford Level 20			
		Time's Pendulum	Alice's Adventures in Wonderland	Jabberwocky and other poems	Great Scientists	Antarctic Ambush	The Call of the Wild	The Raven and other poems	Great Engineers	Time Runs Out	Oliver Twist	For the Fallen and other poems	Great Pioneers
Speaking	Express issues and ideas clearly, using specialist vocabulary and examples				•	•							
	Speak clearly, using formal language and varying expression, tone and volume, to keep listeners interested	•						•				•	
	Explore challenging or contentious issues through sustained role play **												
Listening	Listen carefully to presentations and show understanding of the speakers' conclusions or opinions						•						
	Respond to others with questions and comments which focus on reasons, implications and next steps			•					•	•			•
Collaboration and discussion	Contribute purposefully to group discussion to achieve agreed outcomes			•				•			•		
	Follow up points in group discussions, showing agreement or disagreement giving reasons *		•										
Reading strategies	Use a range of strategies to make meaning from words and sentences, including knowledge of phonics, word roots, word families, syntax, text organisation and prior knowledge of context	•											
	Read complex texts independently for sustained periods *												
	Understand how punctuation can vary and so affect sentence structure and meaning, e.g. I had chocolate(,) cake and cheese for tea				•	•							
	Use a range of strategies for finding information, e.g. skimming for gist, scanning for detail								•	•			•

	Dark Red Book Band / Oxford Level 18				Dark Red+ Book Band / Oxford Level 19				Dark Red+ Book Band / Oxford Level 20			
	Time's Pendulum	Alice's Adventures in Wonderland	Jabberwocky and other poems	Great Scientists	Antarctic Ambush	The Call of the Wild	The Raven and other poems	Great Engineers	Time Runs Out	Oliver Twist	For the Fallen and other poems	Great Pioneers
Comprehension												
Show understanding of main ideas and significant details in different texts on the same topic	•	•		•		•	•	•	•	•	•	•
Infer ideas which are not explicitly stated, e.g. *writers' viewpoints or attitudes*	•		•		•			•	•			
Identify ideas and information that interest them to develop further understanding						•				•		
Collate and make connections, e.g. *prioritising, categorising*, between information and ideas from different sources				•	•							
Response and analysis												
Distinguish between facts, theories and opinions												
Compare the viewpoint of different writers on the same topic, e.g. *rats are fascinating or a menace*		•	•			•	•				•	
Consider whether text is effective in conveying information and ideas											•	•

* NOTE: This objective will be covered in every guided reading session
** NOTE: This objective is best addressed outside of the guided reading session

Links to the Northern Ireland Primary Curriculum

Project X *Origins* supports the aims and objectives of the Northern Ireland Curriculum for Literacy and Language in Key Stage 2, and the development of key skills and capabilities.

Communication across the curriculum

The Northern Ireland Primary Curriculum places communication at the centre of the whole curriculum, emphasizing a need to develop lifelong learning skills. **Project X** *Origins* provides opportunities to develop communication skills in the following ways:

Talking and Listening

The importance of talk and other forms of communication in developing children's literacy and wider social skills is widely recognized. The **Project X** *Origins* books have been designed to stimulate talk and role play, providing plenty of opportunities to explore characters, retell stories, raise and respond to questions, and express opinions. The Guided Reading Notes provide a wealth of opportunities for using talk both as a precursor to successful reading, comprehension, and as a means of ensuring that children become confident individuals and effective contributors. In addition, the follow-up activities offer ideas for pair- and group-work and for drama activities.

Reading

Project X *Origins* supports teachers in delivering the Northern Ireland Primary Curriculum, enabling children to:

- read a range of texts for information, ideas and enjoyment
- use a range of strategies to read with increasing independence
- find, select and use information from a range of sources
- understand and explore ideas, event and features in texts
- use evidence from texts to explain opinions.

Project X *Origins* offers children a wide choice of exciting fiction, poetry and non-fiction books introducing children to a variety of different genres and different ways of presenting information. The **Project X** *Origins* Guided Reading Notes provide explicit opportunities for the development of comprehension strategies before, during and after reading, ensuring children are engaged in using tools for reading, finding and using information, and analysing, evaluating and understanding texts.

Writing

Project X *Origins* includes writing opportunities as part of the follow-up activities for every book, encouraging children to use the knowledge they have developed through in-depth exploration of the text and apply these to their own writing. Photocopiable masters for every book also provide extension activities, including writing opportunities.

Thinking skills and personal capabilities

The collaborative approach of **Project X Origins** guided reading sessions helps children to develop personal skills. They are encouraged to develop self-management skills and the ability to collaborate and interact with others.

The **Project X Origins** character fiction stories present readers with a range of scenarios in which the core characters are faced with problems, challenges and decisions to make. By following the adventures of Max, Cat, Ant and Tiger, readers can learn to empathize with situations and explore their own problem-solving skills.

Cross-curricular skills and a thematic approach

Through the inclusion of cross-curricular activities and links to other subject areas, **Project X Origins** encourages children to develop and apply literacy skills across other curriculum subjects and to become successful learners. The Guided Reading Notes provide a range of follow-up activities, many of which are active and hands-on, to support the practical application of literacy skills in a range of contexts. Further ideas for taking this approach to learning are given on page 70 of this handbook.

Assessment

The continuous cycle of on-going assessment, outlined in the Northern Ireland Primary Curriculum, is supported by the **Project X Origins** formative and summative assessment. The in-built assessment prompts in every set of Guided Reading Notes help teachers track and respond to children's progress, helping to identify and target children's specific developmental needs. For more information on the Oxford Reading Criterion Scale, please see page 83.

> **A note on curricular correlation**
>
> Guided reading offers opportunities to cover a large number of reading and oracy objectives. The **Project X Origins graphic texts** Guided Reading Notes highlight the most relevant objectives from the Northern Ireland Primary Curriculum for each book.
>
> The very nature of guided reading means that many objectives will be covered every time teachers run a session; objectives such as these have not been repeated for each title but are asterisked on the following charts.
>
> It is sometimes the case that there are objectives that would be more appropriate to address outside of the guided reading sessions such as in whole-class teaching. Other objectives may be better met by using non-graphic texts. When objectives such as these occur, they have not been correlated to the Guided Reading Notes. These are also indicated on the following charts.

The Northern Ireland Curriculum:
Primary Language and Literacy Key Stage 2 (Years 4–5)

	Grey Book Band/ Oxford Level 14				Dark Blue Book Band/ Oxford Level 15				Dark Blue Book Band/ Oxford Level 16				Dark Red Book Band/ Oxford Level 17			
	Chasing Birdy	The Wind in the Willows	The Pelican Chorus and other poems	Great Artists	Time Stealer	The Jungle Book	If and other poems	Great Inventors	The Sands of Deception	The Secret Garden	I Wandered Lonely as a Cloud and other poems	Great Naturalists	The Jutchen Recruits	Treasure Island	The Pied Piper of Hamelin	Great Space Explorers
Talking and Listening																
Listen and respond to a range of fiction, poetry, drama and media texts through the use of traditional and digital resources											•			•		
Tell, retell and interpret stories based on memories, personal experiences, literature, imagination and the content of the curriculum																
Share, respond to and evaluate ideas, arguments and points of view and use evidence or reason to justify opinions, actions or proposals	•			•				•							•	
Formulate, give and respond to guidance, directions and instructions			•													
Participate in a range of drama activities across the curriculum **																
Describe and talk about real experiences and imaginary situations and about people, places, events and artefacts		•				•			•							
Identify and ask appropriate questions to seek information, views and feelings							•			•						
Use appropriate quality of speech and voice, speaking audibly and varying register, according to the purpose and audience *					•											
Read aloud, inflecting appropriately, to express thoughts and feelings and emphasise the meaning of what they have read												•	•			•

66

	Grey Book Band/ Oxford Level 14				Dark Blue Book Band/ Oxford Level 15				Dark Blue Book Band/ Oxford Level 16				Dark Red Book Band/ Oxford Level 17			
	Chasing Birdy	The Wind in the Willows	The Pelican Chorus and other poems	Great Artists	Time Stealer	The Jungle Book	It and other poems	Great Inventors	The Sands of Deception	The Secret Garden	I Wandered Lonely as a Cloud and other poems	Great Naturalists	The Jurchen Recruits	Treasure Island	The Pied Piper of Hamelin	Great Space Explorers
Reading																
Extend the range of their reading and develop their own preferences			•		•		•				•		•		•	
Use traditional and digital sources to locate, select, evaluate and communicate information relevant for a particular task **																
Represent their understanding of texts in a range of ways, including visual, oral, dramatic and digital			•		•		•									•
Consider, interpret and discuss texts, exploring the ways in which language can be manipulated in order to affect the reader or engage attention		•				•			•	•		•	•			
Begin to be aware of how different media present information, ideas and events in different ways **	•	•				•										
Justify their responses logically, by inference, deduction and/or reference to evidence within the text									•							
Reconsider their initial response to texts in the light of insight and information which emerge subsequently from their reading				•						•		•		•		
Use a range of cross-checking strategies to read unfamiliar words in texts				•				•								
Use a variety of reading skills for different reading purposes	•							•			•				•	•

* NOTE: This objective will be covered in every guided reading session
** NOTE: This objective is best addressed outside of the guided reading session

The Northern Ireland Curriculum:
Primary Language and Literacy Key Stage 2 (Year 6)

	Dark Red Book Band / Oxford Level 18				Dark Red+ Book Band / Oxford Level 19				Dark Red+ Book Band / Oxford Level 20			
	Time's Pendulum	Alice's Adventures in Wonderland	Jabberwocky and other poems	Great Scientists	Antarctic Ambush	The Call of the Wild	The Raven and other poems	Great Engineers	Time Runs Out	Oliver Twist	For the Fallen and other poems	Great Pioneers
Talking and Listening												
Listen and respond to a range of fiction, poetry, drama and media texts through the use of traditional and digital resources												
Tell, retell and interpret stories based on memories, personal experiences, literature, imagination and the content of the curriculum		•	•									
Share, respond to and evaluate ideas, arguments and points of view and use evidence or reason to justify opinions, actions or proposals	•						•			•		•
Formulate, give and respond to guidance, directions and instructions												
Participate in a range of drama activities across the curriculum **												
Describe and talk about real experiences and imaginary situations and about people, places, events and artefacts						•						
Identify and ask appropriate questions to seek information, views and feelings									•		•	
Use appropriate quality of speech and voice, speaking audibly and varying register, according to the purpose and audience *												
Read aloud, inflecting appropriately, to express thoughts and feelings and emphasise the meaning of what they have read				•	•							

	Dark Red Book Band/ Oxford Level 18				Dark Red+ Book Band/ Oxford Level 19				Dark Red+ Book Band/ Oxford Level 20			
	Time's Pendulum	Alice's Adventures in Wonderland	Jabberwocky and other poems	Great Scientists	Antarctic Ambush	The Call of the Wild	The Raven and other poems	Great Engineers	Time Runs Out	Oliver Twist	For the Fallen and other poems	Great Pioneers
Reading												
Extend the range of their reading and develop their own preferences		●		●		●				●		●
Use traditional and digital sources to locate, select, evaluate and communicate information relevant for a particular task **												
Represent their understanding of texts in a range of ways, including visual, oral, dramatic and digital												
Consider, interpret and discuss texts, exploring the ways in which language can be manipulated in order to affect the reader or engage attention		●	●		●	●	●	●	●		●	
Begin to be aware of how different media present information, ideas and events in different ways **									●			
Justify their responses logically, by inference, deduction and/or reference to evidence within the text	●			●								
Reconsider their initial response to texts in the light of insight and information which emerge subsequently from their reading												
Use a range of cross-checking strategies to read unfamiliar words in texts							●			●	●	
Use a variety of reading skills for different reading purposes	●		●		●			●				●

* NOTE: This objective will be covered in every guided reading session
** NOTE: This objective is best addressed outside of the guided reading session

Cross-curricular opportunities

Making links between curriculum subjects can deepen children's understanding by providing opportunities to enhance their learning in a number of ways:

- It mirrors the way we learn 'naturally', outside school – our learning environment is often holistic, for example, going shopping might involve literacy, maths and geography.

- It helps embed a consistent approach to developing literacy and language across the curriculum, offering opportunities for skills to be practised and applied in different contexts. It provides opportunities for practising skills – so, skills taught in one curriculum area (e.g. skimming, scanning and analyzing data in literacy) can be developed through purposeful use in other areas such as history or science.

- It builds and enriches concepts – by presenting the same or related information in different ways, through different modes of communication or within different contexts.

- It provides opportunities for the application of knowledge within familiar, new and related contexts and supports children in using higher order thinking skills such as reasoning and problem-solving.

- It helps children retain their learning through the repetition of information, actions and skills in different contexts.

- It makes learning enjoyable – cross-curricular learning often feels more meaningful and more fun, so motivation and engagement can be enhanced.

In using cross-curricular themes it is important to recognize that planning is still usually undertaken at subject level to ensure curriculum coverage and continuity. The following pages contain suggestions for a range of activities linked to the wider curriculum, as well as ideas for creating a contextualized learning environment which will encourage children to make their own explorations of a theme through play and other activities. Such activities also encourage children to make direct links between the theme and their own knowledge and experiences.

Cross-curricular opportunities, Oxford Level 14

Project X *Origins graphic texts* provide the following cross-curricular opportunities at this level (there are additional cross-curricular opportunities listed in the Guided Reading Notes):

Book title	Programme of Study	Suggested activities
Chasing Birdy	**Art and Design:** Pupils should be taught about great artists, architects and designers in history.	Ask the children to research one of Leonardo da Vinci's paintings or inventions that particularly interests them, and write two paragraphs explaining what they have chosen and why it is important. Combine the children's pieces into a book or wall display.
	Geography: Locate the world's countries, using maps to focus on Europe.	Show the children a detailed map of Europe, and ask them to find Italy. Then see if they can locate Tuscany, and finally the town of Vinci. Ask them to use the Internet to find out what the countryside is like around Vinci, and compare it with their own locality.
The Wind in the Willows	**Music:** Improvise and compose music for a range of purposes using the inter-related dimensions of music.	Ask the children to choose one of the locations in the story, such as the riverbank or Toad Hall, and improvise a piece of music to convey the atmosphere of the location, using their voices as well as any available instruments.
	PSHE: Prepare pupils at the school for the opportunities, responsibilities and experiences of later life.	Ask the children what they think of the way Toad behaves in the story. Can they list some of the things he does that are against the law, unkind or unfair? Do they think he has changed his ways at the end of the story? Ask them to write a letter to Toad giving him advice to help him change for the better.
The Pelican Chorus *and other poems*	**PE:** Perform dances using a range of movement patterns.	Ask the children to work in a group of four to six, and choose a favourite poem in the collection. Challenge them to make up a dance to go with the poem, and perform it to the class. Can the class guess which poem they chose?
	Computing: Use search technologies effectively, appreciate how results are selected and ranked, and be discerning in evaluating digital content.	Ask the children to research one of the poets featured in the collection, and create a poster or webpage about them. Challenge the children to distinguish between reliable internet sources (such as The Poetry Foundation website) and potentially unreliable ones (such as Wikipedia).
Great Artists	**Art and Design:** Pupils should be taught about great artists, architects and designers in history.	Ask the children to choose their favourite artist featured in the book, and research three artworks by this artist. Ask them to write a paragraph about their chosen artist's life, and a paragraph about each of the artworks they found.
	Science: Identifying differences, similarities or changes related to simple scientific ideas and processes.	Ask the children to find out more about Barbara Hepworth's sculptures. What kinds of material did she use? Why do the children think she chose those materials? Ask them to draw up a list of materials that are good for making sculptures, and materials that would be difficult to use in this way.

Cross-curricular opportunities, Oxford Level 15

Project X *Origins graphic texts* provide the following cross-curricular opportunities at this level (there are additional cross-curricular opportunities listed in the Guided Reading Notes):

Book title	Programme of Study	Suggested activities
Time Stealer	**Geography:** Name and locate counties and cities of the United Kingdom, geographical regions and their identifying human and physical characteristics, key topographical features, and land-use patterns.	Ask the children to find Edington on a map of England (it's near Westbury in Wiltshire). What can they find out, from the map or from other research, about the local countryside? Ask them to draw a map or picture of the Battle of Edington, drawing on what they have found out about the location.
	Science: Observe that some materials change state when they are heated or cooled, and measure or research the temperature at which this happens in degrees Celsius (°C).	Challenge the children to make their own candle clock (instructions can be found for example at www.ehow.com). Ask them to think about the properties of the candle that make it appropriate for use in this kind of clock. Do they think it would be possible to make a similar clock out of any other melting material (chocolate, butter, ice …)?
The Jungle Book	**PE:** Use running, jumping, throwing and catching in isolation and in combination.	Ask the children to choose their favourite animal from the story, and challenge them to move from one side of the hall or playground to the other in role as their animal, using a mixture of running, jumping, crawling, walking, etc. as appropriate. Can the rest of the group guess which animal they have chosen?
	History: Changes in an aspect of social history, such as crime and punishment from the Anglo-Saxons to the present or leisure and entertainment in the 20th Century.	Ask the children to find out about the life of Rudyard Kipling, using books or Internet resources. Challenge them to find at least ten ways in which Kipling's life as a child in the Victorian era would have been different from their lives today.
If and other poems	**PSHE:** Prepare pupils at the school for the opportunities, responsibilities and experiences of later life.	Ask the children to reread the poem 'If'. What do they think about the advice the poem gives? Do they agree with it? Ask them to write a short poem or persuasive paragraph of their own, giving advice on how to live a good life.
	Art and Design: Pupils should be taught to improve their mastery of art and design techniques, including drawing, painting and sculpture with a range of materials.	Ask the children to choose their favourite poem from the collection and create a piece of art to represent it. Encourage them to make appropriate choices of style and materials, from the range that is available to them. Challenge them to think about how they can use their chosen materials to reflect the poem.
Great Inventors	**Design and Technology:** Use research and develop design criteria to inform the design of innovative, functional, appealing products that are fit for purpose, aimed at particular individuals or groups.	Ask the children to work in pairs or threes to come up with an idea for a new invention of their own. They should make a plan for their invention, thinking about the kinds of materials they would need to use and how the invention would work. Ask them to record their ideas on paper or make a presentation to the class.
	Mathematics: Interpret and present discrete and continuous data using appropriate graphical methods, including bar charts and time graphs.	Ask the children to conduct a survey at home or at school, to find out which inventor in the book people think is the most significant. Encourage them to make their survey as wide as possible, and record their findings in an appropriate format, e.g. a bar chart or pie chart.
	Science: Construct a simple series electrical circuit, identifying and naming its basic parts, including cells, wires, bulbs, switches and buzzers.	Ask the children to work in pairs to construct a simple electrical circuit with a bulb. They could experiment with how to make the bulb brighter (by adding more cells). Ask the pairs to create a 'how to' leaflet so that others could recreate their circuit, which should include a clear diagram.

Cross-curricular opportunities, Oxford Level 16

Project X *Origins graphic texts* provide the following cross-curricular opportunities at this level (there are additional cross-curricular opportunities listed in the Guided Reading Notes):

Book title	Programme of Study	Suggested activities
The Sands of Deception	**Music:** Improvise and compose music for a range of purposes using the inter-related dimensions of music.	Ask the children to work in groups to improvise a short piece of music representing the scene where the friends are pitted against the Tick-Tock Man inside Pharaoh Seti's tomb. They could use percussion instruments to represent the Tick-Tock Man coming closer, and other instruments and their voices to represent the friends.
	Geography: Identify the position and significance of latitude, longitude, Equator, Northern Hemisphere, Southern Hemisphere, the Tropics of Cancer and Capricorn, Arctic and Antarctic Circle, the Prime/Greenwich Meridian and time zones.	Challenge the children to find Egypt and the area of the Valley of the Kings on a map or globe. Can they work out (roughly) what latitude and longitude the Valley of the Kings is at? How does this compare with the children's own location? Ask them to find out what time zone Egypt is in, and work out the time difference.
The Secret Garden	**Geography:** Use fieldwork to observe, measure, record and present the human and physical features in the local area using a range of methods, including sketch maps, plans and graphs, and digital technologies.	Arrange a field trip to a large park or garden. Ask the children to observe the main features that make it an appealing outdoor space. They should record their observations with maps, sketches and/or photographs. When they return to the classroom they could present their findings in a book or webpage.
	History: Changes in an aspect of social history, such as crime and punishment from the Anglo-Saxons to the present or leisure and entertainment in the 20th Century.	Ask the children to research what houses were like in the Edwardian era, when this book is set. They could produce a poster or a short report comparing life in a big Edwardian house with life in a modern city house today.
I Wandered Lonely as a Cloud and other poems	**Art and Design:** Pupils should be taught to create sketch books to record their observations and use them to review and revisit ideas.	On a trip to a local area of interest, or in the school grounds, ask children to find something that interests them visually and make a series of sketches of it, trying to record what they see in different ways, from different angles etc. On their return to the classroom they could work some of their ideas up into a picture or sculpture.
	Computing: Use search technologies effectively, appreciate how results are selected and ranked, and be discerning in evaluating digital content.	Ask the children to choose a favourite poem from the collection, and use the Internet to help them find out more about the poet, or about the aspect of nature described in the poem. Remind them to choose reliable sources for their information, and provide references to show which websites and other resources they used in their research.
Great Naturalists	**Design and Technology:** Use research and develop design criteria to inform the design of innovative, functional, appealing products that are fit for purpose, aimed at particular individuals or groups.	Ask the children to design a bird feeder that could be hung outside the classroom window to attract birds. Encourage them to think about the properties the bird feeder needs in order to hold the food so that birds can access it easily. The children could produce their designs on paper, and then go on to make their bird feeders if appropriate.
	History: Pupils should regularly address and sometimes devise historically valid questions about change, cause, similarity and difference, and significance.	Ask the children which of the naturalists in the book they feel has had the biggest impact on the world. Ask them to do some research to find out more about the life of their chosen naturalist, including ways in which their life may have differed from life today.
	Science: Describe the differences in the life cycles of a mammal, an amphibian, an insect and a bird.	Ask the children to look at again at the life and work of Jane Goodall and to research the life cycle of a chimpanzee. They should then compare this life cycle to an animal found in a local environment. What similarities and differences are there?

Cross-curricular opportunities, Oxford Level 17

Project X *Origins graphic texts* provide the following cross-curricular opportunities at this level (there are additional cross-curricular opportunities listed in the Guided Reading Notes):

Book title	Programme of Study	Suggested activities
The Jurchen Recruits	**PSHE:** Prepare pupils at the school for the opportunities, responsibilities and experiences of later life.	Ask the children which of the friends they feel acts like a leader in this story. What special qualities does a good leader need? Ask the children to work in groups to draw up a job advertisement for the ideal team leader.
	PE: Take part in outdoor and adventurous activity challenges both individually and within a team.	Ask the children to design a training routine for the Jurchen army, including jumps, running, press-ups, etc. Then challenge them to see how quickly they can complete the routine themselves.
Treasure Island	**Geography:** Use maps, atlases, globes and digital/computer mapping to locate countries and describe features studied.	Ask the children to use maps to identify a real island that interests them. It could be in Britain, Europe or North or South America. Encourage them to research their chosen island and create an illustrated fact file about it.
	Art and Design: Pupils should be taught to improve their mastery of art and design techniques, including drawing, painting and sculpture with a range of materials.	Ask the children to create their own pirate flag. Encourage them to make their design as scary and effective as possible in the limited space offered by the flag, and to think about how easy it will be to see from a long distance. They could go on to create a full-size flag, or make a model of a pirate ship flying the flag.
The Pied Piper of Hamelin	**History:** Pupils should understand how our knowledge of the past is constructed from a range of sources.	Ask the children to look in the poem for clues that show the story is set in the past. Ask them to think about how we can use stories and poems from the past for clues about how the world has changed. They could write two or three paragraphs of explanation, exploring how the world shown in the poem is different from our world today.
	Music: Pupils should be taught to play and perform in solo and ensemble contexts, using their voices and playing musical instruments with increasing accuracy, fluency, control and expression.	Ask the children to choose one verse from the poem, and set it to music. They could make up a tune to which they can sing the verse, and/or improvise some musical backing for a reading of the verse.
Great Space Explorers	**Design and Technology:** Investigate and analyse a range of existing products.	Ask the children to do some further research into one of the robotic space explorers featured on pages 28–29. Can they find out how their chosen robot explorer works, and what it is made of?
	Science: Pupils should be taught to describe the movement of the Earth, and other planets, relative to the Sun in the solar system.	Ask the children which of the explorers in the book they feel is the most significant in helping us to understand how the Earth and other planets move around the Sun, considering particularly the differing views of Ptolemy, Copernicus and Galileo. To demonstrate their understanding, have them design posters – or build a model – of how we now understand the solar system to work.

Cross-curricular opportunities, Oxford Level 18

Project X *Origins graphic texts* provide the following cross-curricular opportunities at this level (there are additional cross-curricular opportunities listed in the Guided Reading Notes):

Book title	Programme of Study	Suggested activities
Time's Pendulum	**Geography:** Human geography, including: types of settlement and land use, economic activity including trade links, and the distribution of natural resources including energy, food, minerals and water.	Ask the children to find the Netherlands on a map, and locate the city of The Hague. Encourage them to do some Internet research to find out some of the ways in which the use of the land around The Hague has changed since Huygens's time.
	Design and Technology: Generate, develop, model and communicate their ideas through discussion, annotated sketches, cross-sectional and exploded diagrams, prototypes, pattern pieces and computer-aided design.	Ask the children to design their own case for a pendulum clock. Can they make their design appropriate by making sure the clock is protected, and that it can be seen clearly? They could draw an annotated diagram of their design.
Alice's Adventures in Wonderland	**Science:** Recognise the impact of diet, exercise, drugs and lifestyle on the way their bodies function.	In the book, Alice eats and drinks things that make her shrink and grow almost at random. Link this to the way the food we eat helps us to grow, and ask children to draw and annotate a plateful of food that would contain the right nutrients to promote healthy growth.
	PE: Pupils should be taught to perform dances using a range of movement patterns.	Ask the children to work in small groups, and make up a dance to represent the Caucus-race on pages 12–13. Challenge them to incorporate as many different types of movement as they can.
Jabberwocky and other poems	**Music:** Pupils should be taught to appreciate and understand a wide range of high-quality live and recorded music drawn from different traditions and from great composers and musicians.	Give the children the opportunity to listen to several different pieces of orchestral music in different styles. Ask them to choose one that they feel goes well with the atmosphere of 'Jabberwocky', and practise reading the poem along with the music.
	Art and Design: Pupils should be taught to improve their mastery of art and design techniques, including drawing, painting and sculpture with a range of materials.	'Humpty Dumpty's Recitation' ends on a cliffhanger! Ask the children to work in pairs and discuss what they think might happen next. Challenge them to make a picture or collage that shows how the story ends. If they wish, they can write a few more verses for the poem, to go with their picture.
Great Scientists	**Computing:** Use search technologies effectively, appreciate how results are selected and ranked, and be discerning in evaluating digital content.	If the children could go back in time and meet just one of the scientists from this book, which would they choose? Ask them to do some Internet research to find out more about the life and achievements of their chosen scientist. Then ask them to produce a short persuasive presentation using presentation software, to convince others that their chosen scientist was the most interesting.
	Science: Describe how living things are classified into broad groups according to common observable characteristics and based on similarities and differences, including micro-organisms, plants and animals.	Provide the children with images of a number of animals and encourage them to divide them into vertebrates and invertebrates, asking them to explain their choices. You could extend this activity by asking them to break the groups down even further into fish, birds and mammals, for example, and then into herbivores and carnivores.

Cross-curricular opportunities, Oxford Level 19

Project X *Origins graphic texts* provide the following cross-curricular opportunities at this level (there are additional cross-curricular opportunities listed in the Guided Reading Notes):

Book title	Programme of Study	Suggested activities
Antarctic Ambush	**History:** Pupils should regularly address and sometimes devise historically valid questions about change, cause, similarity and difference, and significance.	Ask the children to research Captain Cook's achievements and decide which were the most significant. Ask them to describe some of the ways in which people's views of the world changed after Captain Cook's discoveries. Do they think his discoveries were a good thing or a bad thing, overall?
	Mathematics: Convert between miles and kilometres.	Ask the children to find out approximately how long one of Captain Cook's journeys was in miles, and then convert this into kilometres. As a further challenge, ask them to find out how long the journey took him, and how long a journey of similar length would take today by air. Can they work out the time difference?
The Call of the Wild	**PSHE:** Prepare pupils at the school for the opportunities, responsibilities and experiences of later life.	Ask the children to find out about the work of organizations such as the RSPCA which attempt to prevent cruelty to animals. Ask them to create a short presentation or report on the work of one such charity or organization.
	PE: Pupils should be taught to take part in outdoor and adventurous activity challenges both individually and within a team.	Ask the children to form teams of four, and try having a relay race outside, with the children running on all-fours, as if they were dogs. Then have a relay race in the same teams, but running normally. What is the difference in times?
The Raven and other poems	**Science:** Describe how living things are classified into broad groups according to common observable characteristics and based on similarities and differences, including microorganisms, plants and animals.	Ask the children to research the animals featured in the collection, and decide where each belongs in the classification system. They could then choose their favourite animal from the book, and research and write an illustrated report about it.
	Geography: Locate the world's countries, using maps to focus on Europe (including the location of Russia) and North and South America, concentrating on their environmental regions, key physical and human characteristics, countries, and major cities.	Ask the children to reread 'Snake' and find out where it is set (Sicily). Can they find Sicily on a map of Europe? Challenge them to find out about the climate and landscape of Sicily. Do they think it sounds like a good place to visit? Ask them to write a brief persuasive piece either encouraging or discouraging tourists from visiting.
Great Engineers	**Computing:** Use search technologies effectively, appreciate how results are selected and ranked, and be discerning in evaluating digital content.	Ask the children to choose an engineer from those featured briefly at the end of the book. Challenge them to find appropriate websites to research their chosen engineer's life and work, and create a presentation about it.
	Design and Technology: Understand how key events and individuals in design and technology have helped shape the world.	Ask the children which of the engineers in the book they feel is the most significant. Ask them to justify their choice, doing extra research if necessary to back up their ideas. Ask the children to present their ideas to the class, and then have a vote to decide which engineer the class feels is the most significant of all.
	History: A significant turning point in British history, for example, the first railways or the Battle of Britain.	Ask the children to research the Industrial Revolution, thinking about which of the many inventions from this period most changed the way people lived. Arrange the children into small groups, asking each child to argue the point for their chosen invention being the most influential.

Cross-curricular opportunities, Oxford Level 20

Project X *Origins graphic texts* provide the following cross-curricular opportunities at this level (there are additional cross-curricular opportunities listed in the Guided Reading Notes):

Book title	Programme of Study	Suggested activities
Time Runs Out	**Science:** Recognise that living things have changed over time and that fossils provide information about living things that inhabited the Earth millions of years ago.	If the children could travel back in time to see any dinosaur, which would they choose and why? Ask them to research their chosen dinosaur and create an illustrated fact file about it, drawing on information about the dinosaur that comes from the fossil record.
	Mathematics: Interpret and construct pie charts and line graphs and use these to solve problems.	Ask the children to do a classroom survey to find out which book about Birdy and the micro-friends is the most popular, and present their findings as a pie chart. As an extra challenge, they could also research which books (including others not in the series) are the most popular of all, and present these findings too.
Oliver Twist	**PSHE:** Prepare pupils at the school for the opportunities, responsibilities and experiences of later life.	Ask the children to work in pairs and decide which character is the most villainous. They should then think of some good advice to help this character change his or her ways. The advice could be written as a letter, or children could role-play an interview with the character.
	Geography: Name and locate counties and cities of the United Kingdom, geographical regions and their identifying human and physical characteristics, key topographical features; and understand how some of these aspects have changed over time.	Ask the children to find out about what London was like during the Victorian era, and compare it with London now. How has the city changed? Encourage them to focus on the way land was used in Victorian times and the way it is used today.
For the Fallen and other poems	**Music:** Appreciate and understand a wide range of high-quality live and recorded music drawn from different traditions and from great composers and musicians.	Give the children the opportunity to listen to some music connected to the First World War, such as *The Last Post*, Gustav Holst's *Planets Suite* (particularly 'Mars') or Ivor Gurney's *In Flanders*. Ask them to choose the piece they feel is most evocative, and write a poem or draw a picture of their own in response to it.
	Computing: Use search technologies effectively, appreciate how results are selected and ranked, and be discerning in evaluating digital content.	Ask the children to use search engines to help them find some more poems associated with different wars (for example, the Second World War). They could create their own presentation, blog or webpage giving information about the poems they have found. Remind them to be careful about copyright issues, particularly if publishing the text of poems on the Internet.
Great Pioneers	**History:** A significant turning point in British history, for example, the first railways or the Battle of Britain.	Ask the children to further research the history of television and the impact its invention has on us today. Ask the children to prepare a presentation on their findings.
	Art and Design: Pupils should be taught about great artists, architects and designers in history.	Ask the children to find out about a pioneering artist who changed people's expectations and views about art, such as Pablo Picasso, Andy Warhol or Henri Matisse. They could produce a poster, presentation or report on the work of their chosen artist.

3. Engaging parents and carers

Parental partnership must be part of a whole-school strategy if it is to be effective in improving outcomes for children. Schools should seek to build a relationship of trust between the school and the home that will lead to effective communication.

Research has identified that the quality of the home learning environment has a massive impact on children's progress.

- *Parental involvement in a child's literacy has been reported as a more powerful force than other family background variables, such as social class, family size and level of parental education.* (Flouri and Buchanan, 2004; cited in Clark and Rumbold, 2006).[1]

- *Parents and the home environment are essential to the early teaching of reading and fostering a love of reading; children are more likely to continue to be readers in homes where books and reading are valued.* (Clark and Rumbold, 2006).[2]

When parents/carers and practitioners work together, the results have a positive impact on children's development and learning at home and at school. Washbrook and Waldfogel found that children from poorer backgrounds lag behind their more privileged peers in terms of cognitive development; they also found that activities such as reading to children and having fixed bedtimes can significantly reduce this gap.[3]

[1,2] Education Standards Research Team, *Research evidence on reading for pleasure*, May 2012.
[3] Washbrook, E. and Waldfogel, J., *The Sutton Trust Low income and early cognitive development in the UK*, (2010).

In 2009, Estyn reported that schools which effectively involve parents in supporting improved standards of achievement: offer flexible arrangements for parents' evenings; provide translators for parents who do not speak English; provide parents with clear information about their expectations regarding the homework policy and set appropriate homework with enough information so that parents know how to help; provide parents with a topic or subject sheet outlining the term's work and choose topics where parents could help easily; record stories for parents who do not speak English to follow the book with their child at home; and encourage parents to borrow 'story sacks' to use at home with their children.[1]

Tips

Here are some ways to encourage parents/carers to get involved with their children's reading.

- Share research with parents/carers that shows children who are read to do better in school.

- Invite parents/carers to a meeting about how you teach a specific aspect of reading. As part of the event have a professional storyteller tell a story to encourage parents/carers to tell stories about everyday life to their children.

- Encourage parents/carers to participate in a guided reading session in school.

- Involve parents/carers in running a book exchange of children's and adult books.

- Encourage parents/carers to read books, newspapers and magazines around the home. Use the slogan 'Read by example'. Ask parents/carers to bring in photographs of themselves reading and display them in the school with appropriate captions.

- Suggest parents/carers provide children with books, comics and writing materials in their bedrooms to encourage children to read and write for pleasure.

- Provide parents/carers with a list of books from a range of authors. Regularly 'spotlight' a book in an area to which parents have access.

- Encourage parents/carers and children to join the local library.

On the next page, you will find a sheet of simple tips and practical advice for parents/carers on how to support their child with their reading. This can be photocopied or adapted for your own Home-School programme.

---

[1] Estyn, 'Good Practice in Parental Involvement in Primary Schools', Her Majesty's Inspecorate for Education and Training in Wales: 27. (2009)

Reading with your child

Here are some simple tips to help you help your child with reading at home.

Enjoy it!

- Make book sharing a fun time that you both enjoy – snuggle up with a book!
- Read old favourites together as well as new books.
- If your child reads to you, or joins in when you are reading to them, show them that you are proud of what they can do.

Make time and space!

- Make reading a special part of your day. Try to find a time when you aren't busy doing other things so you can spend 'quality time' reading together – even if it's only for a few minutes.
- Try to find a quiet place away from distractions like the television or the computer.
- Try to find some time every day for reading together – 10 minutes each day is better than a long session once a week.

Be positive!

- Give your child lots of praise, encouragement and support when they read to you. Focus on what they did well, not what they did wrong. Even small successes are important.
- Never force your child – if they are reluctant to read you could offer a small reward such as playing a game they enjoy. If they are tired or very reluctant, read to them instead.

Find out what they like to read!

- Sometimes we read for pleasure but much of the time we read for a reason. Read lots of different things together – stories, information books, comics, magazines, websites, cereal packets, TV listings – anything you and your child enjoy reading or need to read.
- Let your child make his or her own reading choices sometimes. They need to develop their own personal likes and dislikes. It is OK not to like some books! Don't worry if they choose an 'easy' or favourite book over and over again. This is normal and helps children build their reading confidence and enthusiasm.
- Join the local library and let your child choose from the great range of books on offer.

Talk about it!

- Talking about books will help your child become more involved and interested in reading and can help them understand more.
- After you've read a book together – or anything else you choose to read – talk about it. What was it about? How did it make you feel? What did you like or not like about it? What did you learn? Spend some time looking at the pictures and talk about what they tell you. Never cover the pictures while sharing a book.
- You can talk with your child about anything – games, TV programmes, films or other things you do together.

Oxford OWL

For school
Discover eBooks, inspirational resources, advice and support

For home
Helping your child's learning with free eBooks, essential tips and fun activities

www.oxfordowl.co.uk

4. Developing the reading environment

The physical environment plays an important part in building a reading culture in school. Classroom book areas, including role-play areas based on books, can help to encourage reading and support children's learning.

An effective reading environment might include:

- interactive displays promoting different books, perhaps linked to a current theme or curriculum topic, or reading in general
- examples of children's work, including book reviews or recommendations
- opportunities for reading, writing, speaking and listening, including ICT-based opportunities
- good models, learning prompts and resources to support learners in developing their literacy skills
- attractive displays of books, including new stock
- a dedicated space for children to sit and read
- language-rich displays such as alphabets/graphemes, common words, topic words, days of the week/months of the year
- details of reading challenges or competitions that the school are taking part in.

Such an environment could include an attractive book area with support materials and play and drama opportunities, encouraging children to make links between their reading and wider learning.

Role-play areas are often abandoned as children move from the lower to upper primary year groups but those primary classrooms that retain elements of role-play practice, perhaps in the form of a themed area, report that these continue to stimulate creative responses, talk, drama and prompts for writing.

4. Developing the reading environment

A wide range of texts
- Attractive, age-appropriate books, both fiction and non-fiction
- Collections of books linked to the theme/s being studied in class
- Other reading materials including brochures, catalogues, magazines, manuals and so on
- Children's own published writing
- Audio and/or visual texts such as talking stories, films and videos
- Dictionaries, atlases and children's thesauruses
- Audio and audio-visual texts and playback equipment

Themed area
- Related to a theme, a book, or an environment
- Labels, signs and other appropriate environmental text
- Small world figures, toys, construction equipment, puppets and art and design materials to encourage the enactment, animation, extension and creation of settings, stories and information
- Materials for writing

A good reading environment includes ...

Displays
- Posters, charts and so on related to particular books, characters, authors or themes
- Learning prompts such as an alphabet frieze, word lists, learning strategy posters, writing frameworks and so on
- Children's book reviews and other purposeful writing
- Labels, signs and notices for children to read in context

Vocabulary resources
- Word walls, word lists, word webs, word family charts
- Photographs and other images related to new vocabulary
- Word games – Scrabble, Pictionary, word snap
- Word of the Week and topic word displays

A comfy space
- Carpet, mats, an armchair, cushions to make the reading area comfortable and inviting

5. Targeting resources: Oxford Assessment and Levelling

Regular, systematic assessment of children's reading development is essential to the teaching process, helping review children's progress and informing future teaching. **Project X** *Origins* has Oxford Assessment and Levelling at its core, helping teachers to:

- assess every child's reading development to get a good understanding of where they are at that moment, and what they need to do next in order to move on,
- find exactly the right books for each guided reading group, matched to their reading development.

Assessment and the Oxford Reading Criterion Scale

At the heart of Oxford Assessment and Levelling is the Oxford Reading Criterion Scale which describes the reading 'journey' that children make, breaking down children's reading development into small steps so that it is easy to identify the stage children have reached, and to work out what each child needs to do next. The Oxford Reading Criterion Scale is the result of many years' research into children's reading development by Ros Wilson, Sarah Threlkeld-Brown, three schools and former Andrell Education Consultants.

The Oxford Reading Criterion Scale is organized into a series of Standards that map to the primary year groups, from Standard 1 (Reception/P1) through to Standard 7 (Year/P7). Each Standard sets out a number of criteria against which children are assessed.

In this handbook you will find:

- Oxford Reading Criterion Scale assessment chart for Standard 5 on page 86,
- Oxford Reading Criterion Scale assessment chart for Standard 6 on page 88,
- Oxford Reading Criterion Scale assessment chart for Standard 7 on page 90,
- Oxford Reading Criterion Scale and **Project X** *Origins graphic texts* correlation charts on page 92.

Oxford Levels and the Oxford Reading Criterion Scale

While assessment is an important activity in its own right, a good assessment tool (such as the Oxford Reading Criterion Scale) provides you with much more; it is diagnostic and informs the next steps in teaching and learning. The **Project X** *Origins* Guided Reading Notes highlight opportunities to develop and assess the skills identified in the Oxford Reading Criterion Scale and the finely levelled **Project X** *Origins* books ensure teachers have resources that provide just the right amount of practice with key skills, and also allow scope to stretch children's abilities.

Information on how this levelling relates to the **Project X** *Origins graphic texts* books can be found on page 98.

The Oxford Reading Criterion Scale and other assessment and levelling systems

The chart below shows how the Oxford Reading Criterion Scale relates to Oxford Levels and Book Bands. The links between the Oxford Reading Criterion Scale and Book Bands are approximate and are given for general guidance only.

Year Group			Oxford Reading Criterion Scale	Oxford Level	Book Band
Year 4	Year 5	Year 6			
■	▓		Standard 5	14	Grey
■	▓			15	Dark Blue
□	■	▓	Standard 6	16	Dark Blue
□	■	▓		17	Dark Red
□	□	■	Standard 7	18	Dark Red
□	□	■		19	Dark Red +
□	□	■		20	Dark Red +

■	Expected range for majority of children in this year group
□	Normal range for tracking forward for more able readers in this year group
▓	Normal range for tracking back less able readers in this year group

Oxford Primary Reading Assessment

This publication provides detailed guidance on the Oxford Levels, the Oxford Reading Criterion Scale Standard Charts for the whole school (Pre-reading through to Standard 7) and correlation between Oxford Levels, Oxford Reading Criterion Scale Grades and all UK curricula.

For more information visit:
www.oxfordprimary.co.uk

How to use Oxford Assessment and Levelling

Most schools begin using the Oxford Reading Criterion Scale with an initial/ baseline summative assessment. Similar to guided reading sessions, these are known as Comprehension Conversations, and can be done with one child or a group of up to four. (Further support for these can be found in the **Oxford Primary Reading Assessment Handbook**.) It is recommended that summative assessments are done at the end of each term (though some schools prefer a single, end-of-year assessment).

≫ Assess

- Organize children into small groups of no more than four and using your knowledge of the children's reading, select the Oxford Reading Criterion Scale Standard which is most likely to fit each group's current reading development.

- Photocopy the relevant Standard Criteria assessment chart for each child in the group and for each child, look at the criteria in detail and tick any criteria that you are confident they have already attained.

- Prepare for the assessment by selecting a **Project X Origins** book at the appropriate level – this should be a book which you are confident the children can all tackle, but which they have not already read. Look at the criteria which you want to focus on and use the **Project X Origins** Guided Reading Notes to help prepare questions you could ask the children in order to check their reading skills in the context of these criteria.

- Gather the group together and ask them to read part of the chosen book. Sample their reading so that you can assess their word-reading skills and then talk to them about their understanding of the text in order to assess their comprehension.
- Against each of the remaining criteria, put a tick if a child has achieved it, a cross if they have not achieved it, and a dot if the child is 'almost there'.
- Count up the number of ticked criteria and use the box at the bottom of the Standard to make a judgement. As well as showing whether a child is Developing, Secure or Advanced against expectations, the judgement indicates the best Oxford Level for a child to be reading at.

The READ key

The particular reading skill that each criterion is assessing is highlighted in brackets so that teachers can quickly identify general areas of strength or weakness for each child:

- READ = word reading and general reading behaviour
- R = recall and retrieval
- E = exploring the author's language and point of view
- A = analysis, of structure and organization
- D = deduction and inference.

Please note: although the criteria in each Standard are set out in broadly hierarchical order, this is only a general guide – children will not necessarily achieve the skills in the order presented – so it is important to consider and assess each criterion on its own merits regardless of where it appears on the scale.

Following a summative assessment, teachers should make observational notes and ongoing judgements against the criteria on the Oxford Reading Criterion Scale Standard for each child. This can be done during guided reading sessions, when working with children individually or whenever an opportunity arises. This process helps the teacher build up a clear and accurate picture of the progress children are making against expectations and in each of the different skills of reading; it enables teachers to quickly identify and address gaps in children's learning and/or to extend learning as appropriate. At the point of the next summative assessment, teachers only need to focus on those criteria that have not been judged as secure.

Identify

Using the records of individual children's assessments, marked on the Oxford Reading Criterion Scale assessment charts, you can plan future teaching: the criteria marked with a dot are those which children are closest to achieving, and it makes sense to focus on these skills; the criteria marked with a cross represent the skills which children are furthest from acquiring (look carefully at these, as they may include skills from further down the Oxford Reading Criterion Scale which need detailed revision and practice, as well as 'higher' skills which children have not yet begun to acquire).

Choose

Each **Project X Origins** book has a selection of Oxford Reading Criterion Scale criteria embedded within every set of Guided Reading Notes so you can choose exactly the right title to match the skills each child needs to work on next.

Teach and assess

The step-by-step guidance and in-built assessment within every set of **Project X Origins** Guided Reading Notes supports you to target, develop and track children's reading skills and progress.

Oxford Reading Criterion Scale
Standard 5: Year 4/Primary 5

Standard 5 can be used during both formal and informal observations of children as their learning progresses through Year 4/Primary 5. A review of the evidence gathered and a summative assessment of each child is recommended once a term.

By the end of Year 4/Primary 5, children should be able to:

- Independently apply a range of strategies to establish meaning from texts, including skimming and scanning for clues or evidence.
- Read aloud with intonation and expression, taking into account more sophisticated punctuation and presentational devices.
- Summarize and/or explain the main points of a text.
- Use knowledge of text structures to locate information.
- Refer to specific parts of a text in support of thoughts, ideas and opinions.
- Make simple inferences and interpretations based on clues from the text.
- Say how and why a writer has created an impact on the reader.
- Recognize and discuss the work of some well-known writers.

Children are expected to be a Secure Standard 5 – reading at Oxford Level 15 – by the end of Year 4/P5 in order to meet the national expectations at the end of Key Stage 2.

Standard 5: Year 4/Primary 5

Name: Date:

No.	Criteria	Evidence? (✔, ✗, ●)
1	Can read aloud with intonation and expression, taking into account presentational devices (e.g. capital letters or italics for emphasis) and a more sophisticated range of punctuation, including … () – . (READ)	
2	Can read confidently and independently using a range of strategies appropriately to establish meaning, e.g. self-correcting, widening knowledge of vocabulary. (READ)	
3	Can skim read texts to gather the general impression of what has been written. (R)	
4	Can scan texts to locate specific information. (R)	
5	Can use text marking to support retrieval of information or ideas from texts, e.g. highlighting, notes in the margin. (R)	
6	Can summarize and explain main points in a text.	
7	Can refer to the text to support opinions and predictions. (R/D)	
8	Can use clues from action, description and dialogue to help establish meaning. (D)	
9	Can read some Y4/5 high frequency words. (READ)	
10	Can use knowledge of text structure to locate information, e.g. use appropriate heading and sub-heading in non-fiction, find relevant paragraph or chapter in fiction. (A)	
11	Can identify the ways in which paragraphs are linked, e.g. use of connecting adverbs or pronouns for character continuity. (A)	
12	Is able to quote directly from the text to support thoughts and discussions. (R)	
13	Can work out the meanings of ambitious words and/or phrases in context. (D)	
14	Can read between the lines, using clues from action, dialogue and description to interpret meaning and/or explain what characters are thinking or feeling and the way they act. (D)	

15	Is beginning to explore potential alternatives that could have occurred in texts (e.g. a different ending), referring to text to justify their ideas. (D)	
16	Can identify the point of view from which a story is told. (D)	
17	Can identify the effects of different words and phrases to create different images and atmosphere, e.g. powerful verbs, descriptive adjectives and adverbs. (E)	
18	Can identify the author's choice of language and its effect on the reader in non-fiction texts (e.g. 'foul felon' in a newspaper report about a burglary). (E)	
19	Can sometimes discuss how a text can affect the reader and the language the author has used to create those feelings. (E)	
20	Can discuss the work of some established authors and knows what is special about their work. (E)	
21	Is beginning to identify differences between some different fiction genres. (A)	
22	Is beginning to recognize how a character is presented in different ways and respond to this with reference to the text. (D)	
23	Can sometimes explain different characters' points of view. (D)	
24	Can compare the structure of different stories to discover how they differ in pace, build up, sequence, complication and resolution. (A)	

Assessment score

0–5 ticks = not yet working at this Standard; review against Standard 4
6–12 ticks = Developing (Oxford Level 14)
13–19 ticks = Secure (Oxford Level 15)
20–23 ticks = Advanced (Oxford Level 16)
Assessment point: children with 21 or more ticks may be assessed against Standard 6.

Oxford Reading Criterion Scale
Standard 6: Year 5/Primary 6

Standard 6 can be used during both formal and informal observations of children as their learning progresses through Year 5/Primary 6. A review of the evidence gathered and a summative assessment of each child is recommended once a term.

By the end of Year 5/Primary 6, children should be able to:

- Clarify the meaning of words in different contexts.
- Skim and scan texts efficiently to identify and retrieve information.
- Identify and discuss a range of fiction genres and share views and recommendations.
- Compare and discuss information and/or ideas within and across texts.
- Use inference and deduction to explore plot, character and mood and in more depth.
- Identify and discuss the use of imagery in texts.
- Justify and elaborate on thoughts and opinions, referring back to the text.
- Recognize and discuss the appeal of some classic texts.

Children are expected to be a Secure Standard 6 – reading at Oxford Level 17 – by the end of Year 5/P6 in order to meet national expectations at the end of Key Stage 2.

STANDARD 6: Year 5/Primary 6

Name: Date:

No.	Criteria	Evidence? (✓, ✗, ●)
1	Can read aloud with pace, fluency and expression, taking into account a wide range of presentational devices and punctuation. (READ)	
2	Can clarify the meaning of unknown words from the way they are used in context. (D)	
3	Can skim and scan to identify key ideas in a text. (R)	
4	Can locate and retrieve relevant information and key ideas from different points in a text and across a range of texts, using techniques such as text marking and using contents or index. (R/A)	
5	Can explore potential alternatives that could have occurred in texts (e.g. a different ending), referring to text to justify their ideas. (D)	
6	Can summarize and explain the main points in a text, referring back to the text to support and clarify summaries. (R)	
7	Can identify some features of different fiction genres, e.g. science fiction, adventure, mystery etc. (A)	
8	Can use inference and deduction skills to discuss messages, moods, feelings and attitudes using the clues from the text. (D)	
9	Can identify the point of view from which a story is told. (D)	
10	Can compare and discuss the structures and features of a range of non-fiction texts. (A)	
11	Can discuss how an author builds a character through dialogue, action and description. (D)	
12	Can talk with friends about texts and listen to the opinions of others in order to share text recommendations and widen understanding of the world. (E)	
13	Can discuss how a text may affect the reader and refer back to the text to back up a point of view. (E)	
14	Can identify and discuss where figurative language creates images. (E)	
15	Can read all the Y4/5 high frequency words. (READ)	
16	Can infer and deduce meaning based on evidence drawn from different points in the text. (D)	

17	Can distinguish between fact and opinion. (E)	
18	Can read between the lines, using clues from action, dialogue and description to interpret meaning and explain how and why characters are acting, thinking or feeling. (D)	
19	Can justify and elaborate on thoughts, feelings, opinions and predictions, referring back to the text for evidence. (R/D)	
20	Can compare and discuss different texts to discover how they are similar and how they differ in terms of character, setting, plot, structure and themes. (E/A)	
21	Can justify preferences in terms of authors' styles and themes. (E)	
22	Can decide on the quality and usefulness of a range of texts and explain clearly to others. (R/A)	
23	Can identify why a long-established novel, poem or play may have retained its lasting appeal. (E)	
24	Can discuss the difference between literal and figurative language and the effects on imagery. (E)	
25	Can sometimes recognize the use of irony and comment on the writer's intention (e.g. sarcasm, insincerity, mockery). (E)	
26	Can recognize some text features within some mixed-genre texts. (A)	

Assessment score

0–5 ticks = not yet working at this Standard; review against Standard 5
6–12 ticks = Developing (Oxford Level 16)
13–21 ticks = Secure (Oxford Level 17)
22–26 ticks = Advanced (Oxford Level 18)
Assessment point: children with 23 or more ticks may be assessed against Standard 7.

Oxford Reading Criterion Scale

Standard 7: Year 6/Primary 7

Standard 7 can be used during both formal and informal observations of children as their learning progresses through Year 6/Primary 7. A review of the evidence gathered and a more formal observation of each child is recommended once a term.

By the end of Year 6/Primary 7, children should be able to:

- Work out the meaning of unknown words using a range of strategies.
- Read aloud with appropriate pace and expression.
- Retrieve information from within and across texts to support ideas and opinions.
- Understand and explain how point of view impacts on the reader.
- Confidently infer and deduce meaning based on evidence from the text and using wider knowledge and experience.
- Identify and explain the different structural devices and features a writer has used.
- Comment on the success – or otherwise – of a text in achieving the writer's intention, referring to both structure and language choices.
- Evaluate the relative importance of characters, events or information in a text.

Children who are a Secure Standard 7 – reading at Oxford Level 19 – by the end of Year 6/P7 should meet the national expectations at the end of Key Stage 2.

STANDARD 7: Year 6/Primary 7

Name: Date:

No.	Criteria	Evidence? (✔, ✘, ●)
1	Can work out the meaning of unknown words and phrases by relating to known vocabulary as well as from the way they are used in context. (D)	
2	Can read aloud with pace, fluency and expression, taking punctuation, presentation and author's intent into account. (READ)	
3	Can confidently skim and scan non-fiction texts to speed up research. (R)	
4	Can refer back to the text to support predictions, thoughts and opinions, being able to elaborate in order to provide reasoned justifications. (R/D)	
5	Can recognize text features within mixed-genre texts. (A)	
6	Can identify and discuss features of fiction genres, e.g. science fiction, adventure, mystery etc. (A)	
7	Can identify the point of view of some texts and how this impacts on the reader. (D/E)	
8	Can summarize information from different points in the same text or across a range of texts. (R)	
9	Can clearly identify and retrieve relevant points and key ideas from different points in a text and across a range of texts. (R)	
10	Can use quotations and text references to support ideas and arguments. (R/D)	
11	Can explain a character's motives throughout a text and use evidence from the text to back up opinions. (D)	
12	Can confidently infer and deduce meaning based on evidence drawn from different points in the text and wider experiences. (D)	
13	Can recognize which character the writer wants the reader to like or dislike. (E/D)	
14	Can identify and discuss implicit and explicit points of view in texts, referring back to the text to support thoughts and ideas. (D)	
15	Can comment on the success of a text providing evidence that refers to language, theme and style. (E)	

Oxford Reading Criterion Scale © Oxford University Press. Copying permitted within purchasing school only.

16	Can recognize the use of irony and comment on the writer's intention (e.g. sarcasm, insincerity, mockery). (E)	
17	Can reflect on the wider consequences or significance of information, ideas or events in the text as a whole (e.g. how one small incident altered the whole course of the story). (D)	
18	Can investigate texts to confirm and justify reasoned predictions and opinions. (R/D)	
19	Can explain how the structural choices support the writer's theme or purpose (e.g. in fiction, decisions about plot structure, character development or flash backs/flash forwards; in non-fiction, looking at how a writer organizes information so that the reader can compare/contrast ideas, and devices and decisions the writer has made in multi-genre texts). (A)	
20	Can evaluate relationships between characters, (e.g. how characters behave in different ways as they interact with different people and/or different settings and consider the relative importance of these instances when evaluating a character's actions) referring back to the text to support thoughts and judgements. (D)	
21	Can explain how the author has used different language features (e.g. figurative language, vocabulary choice, use of specific grammatical convention) and the effect of these on the reader. (E)	
22	Can unpick the details of the different layers of meaning in texts, e.g. children use language to discuss texts such as: "This could be interpreted as …", "On the other hand …", "Perhaps the writer is suggesting …", "One way of looking at this is that … whilst another could be …". (D)	

Assessment score

Assessment score
0–5 ticks = not yet working at this Standard; review against Standard 6
6–11 ticks = Developing (Oxford Level 18)
12–19 ticks = Secure (Oxford Level 19)
20–23 ticks = Advanced (Oxford Level 20)

Links to the Oxford Reading Criterion Scale: Standard 5

	Grey Book Band/Oxford Level 14			Dark Blue Book Band/Oxford Level 15				
	Chasing Birdy	The Wind in the Willows	The Pelican Chorus and other poems	Great Artists	Time Stealer	The Jungle Book	If and other poems	Great Inventors
1. Can read aloud with intonation and expression, taking into account presentational devices (e.g. capital letters or italics for emphasis) and a more sophisticated range of punctuation, including … ( ) – . (READ)			•		•		•	
2. Can read confidently and independently using a range of strategies appropriately to establish meaning, e.g. self-correcting, widening knowledge of vocabulary. (READ)						•		
3. Can skim read texts to gather the general impression of what has been written. (R)				•				
4. Can scan texts to locate specific information. (R)	•	•			•	•		•
5. Can use text marking to support retrieval of information or ideas from texts, e.g. highlighting, notes in the margin. (R) **								•
6. Can summarize and explain main points in a text.	•	•	•	•		•		•
7. Can refer to the text to support opinions and predictions. (R/D)	•			•			•	•
8. Can use clues from action, description and dialogue to help establish meaning. (D)	•			•	•		•	
9. Can read some Y4/5 high frequency words. (READ) *								
10. Can use knowledge of text structure to locate information, e.g. use appropriate heading and sub-heading in non-fiction, find relevant paragraph or chapter in fiction. (A)								•
11. Can identify the ways in which paragraphs are linked, e.g. use of connecting adverbs or pronouns for character continuity. (A) **				•	•			
12. Is able to quote directly from the text to support thoughts and discussions. (R)		•	•	•				•
13. Can work out the meanings of ambitious words and/or phrases in context. (D)			•	•	•			
14. Can read between the lines, using clues from action, dialogue and description to interpret meaning and/or explain what characters are thinking or feeling and the way they act. (D)	•				•	•		•

	Grey Book Band/Oxford Level 14				Dark Blue Book Band/Oxford Level 15			
	Chasing Birdy	The Wind in the Willows	The Pelican Chorus and other poems	Great Artists	Time Stealer	The Jungle Book	If and other poems	Great Inventors
15. Is beginning to explore potential alternatives that could have occurred in texts (e.g. a different ending), referring to text to justify their ideas. (D)								
16. Can identify the point of view from which a story is told. (D)					•		•	
17. Can identify the effects of different words and phrases to create different images and atmosphere, e.g. powerful verbs, descriptive adjectives and adverbs. (E)			•				•	
18. Can identify the author's choice of language and its effect on the reader in non-fiction texts (e.g. 'foul felon' in a newspaper report about a burglary). (E)								•
19. Can sometimes discuss how a text can affect the reader and the language the author has used to create those feelings. (E)		•	•			•		
20. Can discuss the work of some established authors and knows what is special about their work. (E)					•	•		
21. Is beginning to identify differences between some different fiction genres. (A)								
22. Is beginning to recognize how a character is presented in different ways and respond to this with reference to the text. (D)	•	•						
23. Can sometimes explain different characters' points of view. (D)		•		•		•		
24. Can compare the structure of different stories to discover how they differ in pace, build up, sequence, complication and resolution. (A) **								

* NOTE: This objective will be covered in every guided reading session
** NOTE: This objective is best addressed outside of the guided reading session

Links to the Oxford Reading Criterion Scale: Standard 6

	Dark Blue Book Band/Oxford Level 15			Dark Red Book Band/Oxford Level 16		Dark Red Book Band/Oxford Level 17	
	The Sands of Deception	The Secret Garden	I Wandered Lonely as a Cloud and other poems	Great Naturalists	The Jurchen Recruits	Treasure Island	The Pied Piper of Hamelin	Great Space Explorers
1. Can read aloud with pace, fluency and expression, taking into account a wide range of presentational devices and punctuation. (READ)							•	•
2. Can clarify the meaning of unknown words from the way they are used in context. (D)		•	•			•	•	
3. Can skim and scan to identify key ideas in a text. (R)	•				•			
4. Can locate and retrieve relevant information and key ideas from different points in a text and across a range of texts, using techniques such as text marking and using contents or index. (R/A) **	•							
5. Can explore potential alternatives that could have occurred in texts (e.g. a different ending), referring to text to justify their ideas. (D)	•							
6. Can summarize and explain the main points in a text, referring back to the text to support and clarify summaries. (R)	•			•	•	•	•	•
7. Can identify some features of different fiction genres, e.g. science fiction, adventure, mystery etc. (A) **		•	•					
8. Can use inference and deduction skills to discuss messages, moods, feelings and attitudes using the clues from the text. (D)				•				
9. Can identify the point of view from which a story is told. (D)					•			
10. Can compare and discuss the structures and features of a range of non-fiction texts. (A)	•	•		•		•		•
11. Can discuss how an author builds a character through dialogue, action and description. (D)				•	•			
12. Can talk with friends about texts and listen to the opinions of others in order to share text recommendations and widen understanding of the world. (E) *		•	•				•	
13. Can discuss how a text may affect the reader and refer back to the text to back up a point of view. (E)		•						
14. Can identify and discuss where figurative language creates images. (E)			•					
15. Can read all the Y4/5 high frequency words. (READ) *								

	Dark Blue Book Band/Oxford Level 16			Dark Red Book Band/Oxford Level 17			
	The Sands of Deception	The Secret Garden	I Wandered Lonely as a Cloud and other poems	Great Naturalists	The Jurchen Recruits	Treasure Island	The Pied Piper of Hamelin	Great Space Explorers
16. Can infer and deduce meaning based on evidence drawn from different points in the text. (D)	•	•		•	•			•
17. Can distinguish between fact and opinion. (E)								
18. Can read between the lines, using clues from action, dialogue and description to interpret meaning and explain how and why characters are acting, thinking or feeling. (D)	•	•		•	•			
19. Can justify and elaborate on thoughts, feelings opinions and predictions, referring back to the text for evidence. (R/D)						•		
20. Can compare and discuss different texts to discover how they are similar and how they differ in terms of character, setting, plot, structure and themes. (E/A)			•			•		•
21. Can justify preferences in terms of authors' styles and themes. (E)			•					
22. Can decide on the quality and usefulness of a range of texts and explain clearly to others. (R/A) **								
23. Can identify why a long-established novel, poem or play may have retained its lasting appeal. (E)			•			•	•	
24. Can discuss the difference between literal and figurative language and the effects on imagery. (E)			•				•	
25. Can sometimes recognize the use of irony and comment on the writer's intention (e.g. sarcasm, insincerity, mockery). (E)						•		
26. Can recognize some text features within some mixed-genre texts. (A)								•

* NOTE: This objective will be covered in every guided reading session
** NOTE: This objective is best addressed outside of the guided reading session

Links to the Oxford Reading Criterion Scale: Standard 7

	Dark Red Book Band / Oxford Level 18				Dark Red+ Book Band / Oxford Level 19				Dark Red+ Book Band / Oxford Level 20			
	Time's Pendulum	Alice's Adventures in Wonderland	Jabberwocky and other poems	Great Scientists	Antarctic Ambush	The Call of the Wild	The Raven and other poems	Great Engineers	Time Runs Out	Oliver Twist	For the Fallen and other poems	Great Pioneers
1. Can work out the meaning of unknown words and phrases by relating to known vocabulary as well as from the way they are used in context. (D)		•					•				•	
2. Can read aloud with pace, fluency and expression, taking punctuation, presentation and author's intent into account. (READ)			•				•				•	•
3. Can confidently skim and scan non-fiction texts to speed up research. (R)				•								
4. Can refer back to the text to support predictions, thoughts and opinions, being able to elaborate in order to provide reasoned justifications. (R/D)		•		•	•		•	•		•		•
5. Can recognize text features within mixed-genre texts. (A)					•			•				
6. Can identify and discuss features of fiction genres, e.g. science fiction, adventure, mystery etc. (A)				•								
7. Can identify the point of view of some texts and how this impacts on the reader. (D/E)											•	
8. Can summarize information from different points in the same text or across a range of texts. (R)											•	
9. Can clearly identify and retrieve relevant points and key ideas from different points in a text and across a range of texts. (R)				•		•						
10. Can use quotations and text references to support ideas and arguments. (R/D)	•	•	•	•		•	•	•	•	•		
11. Can explain a character's motives throughout a text and use evidence from the text to back up opinions. (D)	•	•	•						•	•		
12. Can confidently infer and deduce meaning based on evidence drawn from different points in the text and wider experiences. (D)		•		•								
13. Can recognize which character the writer wants the reader to like or dislike. (E/D)	•					•						•
14. Can identify and discuss implicit and explicit points of view in texts, referring back to the text to support thoughts and ideas. (D)			•							•	•	
15. Can comment on the success of a text providing evidence that refers to language, theme and style. (E)										•	•	•

	Dark Red Book Band / Oxford Level 18				Dark Red+ Book Band / Oxford Level 19				Dark Red+ Book Band / Oxford Level 20			
	Time's Pendulum	Alice's Adventures in Wonderland	Jabberwocky and other poems	Great Scientists	Antarctic Ambush	The Call of the Wild	The Raven and other poems	Great Engineers	Time Runs Out	Oliver Twist	For the Fallen and other poems	Great Pioneers
16. Can recognize the use of irony and comment on the writer's intention (e.g. sarcasm, insincerity, mockery). (E)					•							
17. Can reflect on the wider consequences or significance of information, ideas or events in the text as a whole (e.g. how one small incident altered the whole course of the story). (D)	•				•	•			•			
18. Can investigate texts to confirm and justify reasoned predictions and opinions. (R/D)	•								•			
19. Can explain how the structural choices support the writer's theme or purpose (e.g. in fiction, decisions about plot structure, character development or flash backs/flash forwards; in non-fiction, looking at how a writer organizes information so that the reader can compare/ contrast ideas, and devices and decisions the writer has made in multigenre texts). (A)			•		•		•	•	•	•	•	
20. Can evaluate relationships between characters. (e.g. how characters behave in different ways as they interact with different people and/or different settings and consider the relative importance of these instances when evaluating a character's actions) referring back to the text to support thoughts and judgements. (D)	•	•			•	•				•		
21. Can explain how the author has used different language features (e.g. figurative language, vocabulary choice, use of specific grammatical convention) and the effect of these on the reader. (E)		•					•	•	•		•	•
22. Can unpick the details of the different layers of meaning in texts, e.g. children use language to discuss texts such as: "This could be interpreted as ...", "On the other hand ...", "Perhaps the writer is suggesting ...", "One way of looking at this is that ... whilst another could be ...". (D)							•					

Oxford Levelling

The **Project X** *Origins* books are finely levelled using Oxford's rigorous levelling criteria. The criteria pay close attention to the surface and structural features of a text, such as use of punctuation, and also look at factors which enhance children's enjoyment of books, such as character and plot progression. In this way, as well as developing reading skills and stamina, children also develop a real enthusiasm for books. This enthusiasm, coupled with effective teaching, will help children become skilful and expert readers by the time they leave Year 6/P7.

Levelling and graphic texts

It's important to remember that where there is less text on the page, a reader needs to work much harder in terms of inference. This is certainly the case with **Project X** *Origins graphic texts*. As children progress through the Oxford Levels, the level of inference required to comprehend the books becomes much higher. Visual literacy – the interaction between the images, and between the images and the text – is key to ensuring children's comprehension. With graphic texts, the text is integrated with the visuals, so they have a truly symbiotic relationship.

The pages that follow give an overview as to how the levelling works within **Project X** *Origins graphic texts*. However, it's important to bear in mind the requirements of the different book 'types'. For example, the Poetry books depend upon the original poem text – any differentiation in levelling comes from the number of frames upon the page and the overall complexity of the poems and subject matter. The Classics may feature more archaic language and the Non-fiction books will inevitably require the use of more technical language at the higher levels. In contrast, the characters in the Character fiction stories tend to use more naturalistic language and speak in a way that is familiar to the reader. In the Character fiction books, differences in levelling centre on features such as increasing plot complexity, use of sub-plots, increasingly sophisticated language in the narrative text boxes, etc.

Poetry

In general the complexity of the poems increases in terms of content, subject matter and language demands as you go through the levels. The images support the text by creating a narrative flow through the poems. There may be fewer frames on some of the poetry spreads which is dictated by where the line and stanza breaks are.

For the Fallen and other poems (Oxford Level 20)

Oxford Level 14 (Grey Book Band)

Chasing Birdy (Oxford Level 14)

What texts are like

- Plots mostly follow a linear pattern, but characters may reflect on past events outside the story timeframe,
- Themes may run across the whole book that are not explicitly signalled in the text, but are relatively easy for readers to work out,
- Readers may be expected to piece together information or evidence across a whole book.

Frames

- 3-10 frames per double-page spread (average 8),
- Most frames contain some text. If a frame doesn't have text in, it is for a particular reason, i.e. the meaning can be better conveyed through artwork alone.

Sentences

- Mostly straightforward sentence structures in both caption boxes and speech bubbles. The sentences are structured in a way that's predictable and easy to follow – e.g. not too many inverted structures or unusual syntax. Following the sentence grammar should not depend too much on inference,
- Links between text that continues between caption boxes and/or speech/thought bubbles are clear for the reader to follow,
- Mainly short, punchy sentences, with a few longer sentences for variety.

Language

- Some challenging vocabulary, but not too many words that require looking up in a dictionary,
- Children should be able to use inference and the story context/artwork to figure out any unknown words,
- Classics: feature key words and phrases using language from the original where appropriate,
- Character fiction: feature speech-like language appropriate to the characters; caption boxes give an opportunity for more some more varied/literary/descriptive language,
- Non-fiction: speech bubble text is mostly naturalistic and predictable, with mostly familiar vocabulary; technical/subject-appropriate vocabulary may appear in caption boxes and speech bubbles as long as the meaning is clear in context.

Inference

- On the whole the reader should be able to make meaning of what's on the page without relying too much on external knowledge. There can be some gaps in the storytelling/leaps between frames for the reader to fill in by inference, as long as the meaning is clear in context.

Oxford Level 15 (Dark Blue Book Band)

Great Inventors (Oxford Level 15)

What texts are like

- Storylines are more complex, involving sub-plots or parallel settings, and stories may not always be straightforwardly linear,
- Themes may run across the whole book that are not explicitly signalled in the text, but are relatively easy for readers to work out,
- Expectations may sometimes be deliberately set up to be subverted,
- Readers may be expected to piece together information or evidence across a whole book.

Frames
- 3-11 frames per double-page spread (average 9),
- Most frames contain some text. If a frame doesn't have text in, it is for a particular reason, i.e. the meaning can be better conveyed through artwork alone.

Sentences
- Mostly straightforward sentence structures in both caption boxes and speech bubbles. Most sentences are structured in a way that's predictable and easy to follow but some might have inverted structures, multiple clauses etc. Following the sentence grammar should not depend too much on inference,
- Links between text that continues between caption boxes and/or speech/thought bubbles are clear for the reader to follow. Connected caption boxes may be interrupted by short speech bubbles,
- Variety in sentence length, with a few longer sentences for variety.

Language
- Some challenging vocabulary, including some words that may require looking up in a dictionary,
- Classics: feature key words and phrases using language from the original where appropriate,
- Character fiction: feature speech-like language appropriate to the characters; caption boxes give an opportunity for some more varied/literary/descriptive language,
- Non-fiction: technical/subject-appropriate vocabulary may appear in caption boxes and speech bubbles as long as the meaning is clear in context.

Inference
- On the whole the reader should be able to make meaning of what's on the page without relying too much on external knowledge. There can be some gaps in the storytelling/leaps between frames for the reader to fill in by inference, as long as the meaning is clear in context.

Oxford Level 16 (Dark Blue Book Band)

The Secret Garden (Oxford Level 16)

What texts are like

- Storylines are more complex, involving sub-plots or parallel settings, and stories may not always be straightforwardly linear,
- Themes may run across the whole book that are not explicitly signalled in the text, but are relatively easy for readers to work out,
- Expectations may sometimes be deliberately set up to be subverted.

Frames
- 3-12 frames per double-page spread (average 10),
- Most frames contain some text. If a frame doesn't have text in, it is for a particular reason, i.e. the meaning can be better conveyed through artwork alone.

Sentences
- A variety of sentence lengths and structures in both caption boxes and speech bubbles, ensuring children encounter a range of styles and giving the text a more sophisticated feel but ensuring the structure supports the meaning of the sentence,
- Sentences may occasionally leave a word out deliberately for the reader to 'fill in', e.g. in the sentence 'The rules allow us not to, but we do', the reader has to use inference and recall the content of a previous sentence to work out what is being referred to,
- Links between text that continues between caption boxes and/or speech/thought bubbles are clear for the reader to follow. Connected caption boxes may be interrupted by short speech bubbles.

Language
- Some challenging vocabulary, appropriate to the context,
- Classics: feature an increasing range of key words and phrases using language from the original,
- Character fiction: feature speech-like language appropriate to the characters; caption boxes give an opportunity for more some more varied/literary/descriptive language,
- Non-fiction: speech bubble and caption text may use more varied language, to convey a character's speech and using technical language appropriate to the topic of the book.

Inference
- More thought and inference may be required from the reader from time to time, to understand what is happening – the action may not always be completely clear on a frame-by-frame basis, so children will need to remember details and carry thoughts from one page/spread to another in order to understand what is happening. The text and artwork may play more tricks on the reader now, beginning to do things such as withholding information, but never with the intention of being deliberately obscure or puzzling.

Oxford Level 17 (Dark Red Book Band)

Treasure Island (Oxford Level 17)

What texts are like

- Storylines are more complex, involving sub-plots or parallel settings, and stories may not always be straightforwardly linear,
- Themes may run across the whole book but not be explicitly signalled,
- The reader may be temporarily misled and information slowly revealed.

Frames

- 3-13 frames per double-page spread (average 11),
- Most frames contain some text. If a frame doesn't have text in, it is for a particular reason, i.e. the meaning can be better conveyed through artwork alone.

Sentences

- An increasing variety of sentence lengths and structure in both caption boxes and speech bubbles, ensuring children encounter a range of styles and giving the text a more sophisticated feel but ensuring the structure supports the meaning of the sentence,
- Sentences may occasionally leave a word out deliberately for the reader to 'fill in', e.g. in the sentence 'The rules allow us not to, but we do', the reader has to use inference and recall the content of a previous sentence to work out what is being referred to,
- Links between text that continues between caption boxes and/or speech/thought bubbles are clear for the reader to follow. Connected caption boxes may be interrupted by speech bubbles and sometimes there may be more than one frame's gap between the first connected box and the second.

Language

- Some challenging vocabulary – not just words children may not know how to use in speech themselves, but words they may not be able to work out using context clues and their knowledge of other words,
- Classics: feature increasing numbers of key words and phrases using language from the original,
- Character fiction: feature speech-like language appropriate to the characters; caption boxes give an opportunity for more some more varied/literary/descriptive language,
- Non-fiction: speech bubble and caption text may use more varied language, to convey a character's speech and using technical language appropriate to the topic of the book.

Inference

- More thought and inference may be required from the reader from time to time, to understand what is happening – the action may not always be completely clear on a frame-by-frame basis, so children will need to remember details and carry thoughts from one page/spread to another in order to understand what is happening. The text and artwork may play more tricks on the reader now, beginning to do things such as withholding information, but never with the intention of being deliberately obscure or puzzling.

Oxford Level 18 (Dark Red Book Band)

Time's Pendulum (Oxford Level 18)

What texts are like

- Storylines are more complex, involving sub-plots or parallel settings, and stories may not always be straightforwardly linear,
- Themes may run across the whole book but not be explicitly signalled in the text,
- The reader may be temporarily misled and information slowly revealed.

Frames
- 3-14 frames per double-page spread (average 12),
- Most frames contain some text. If a frame doesn't have text in, it is for a particular reason, i.e. the meaning can be better conveyed through artwork alone.

Sentences
- An increasing variety of sentence lengths and structure in both caption boxes and speech bubbles, ensuring children encounter a range of styles and giving the text a more sophisticated feel. There should be the same complexity of tone and structure as children would find in a novel at this level,
- Speech or narrative often continues across more than one caption box/speech bubble or frame. Connected caption boxes may be interrupted by speech bubbles and sometimes there may be more than one frame's gap between the first connected box and the second.

Language
- Some challenging vocabulary is expected,
- Classics: often feature key words and phrases in the language of the original,
- Character fiction: feature speech-like language appropriate to the characters; characters from different times and cultures may use a variety of speech styles; caption boxes give an opportunity for more some more varied/literary/descriptive language,
- Non-fiction: speech bubble and caption text may use more varied language, to convey a character's speech and using technical language appropriate to the topic of the book.

Inference
- Books can be structured in a less linear way, and more thought and inference is often required from the reader, to understand what is happening. The text and artwork may play more tricks on the reader now, beginning to do things such as withholding information, so the reader has to work harder to grasp the full meaning.

Oxford Level 19 (Dark Red+ Book Band)

Great Engineers (Oxford Level 19)

What texts are like

- Storylines are more complex, involving sub-plots or parallel settings, and stories may not always be straightforwardly linear,
- There may be themes or underlying ideas in a text which are not superficially obvious,
- Texts may draw on unfamiliar contexts.

Frames

- 2-15 frames per double-page spread (average 13),
- Most frames contain some text. If a frame doesn't have text in, it is for a particular reason, i.e. the meaning can be better conveyed through artwork alone.

Sentences

- An increasing variety of sentence lengths and structure in both caption boxes and speech bubbles to reflect the complexity of tone and structure found in novels at this level,
- Speech or narrative often continues across more than one caption box/speech bubble or frame. Connected caption boxes may be interrupted by speech bubbles and sometimes there may be more than one frame's gap between the first connected box and the second.

Language

- Some challenging vocabulary is welcomed and expected,
- Classics: feature key words and phrases in the language of the original,
- Character fiction: feature speech-like language appropriate to the characters; characters from different times and cultures may use a variety of speech styles; caption boxes give an opportunity for more some more varied/literary/descriptive language as found in novels at this level,
- Non-fiction: speech bubble and caption text use widely varied language, to convey a character's speech and using technical language appropriate to the topic of the book.

Inference

- Books can be structured in a less linear way, and more thought and inference is often required from the reader, to understand what is happening. The text and artwork may play more tricks on the reader now, e.g. sometimes withholding information or setting up temporary false expectations, so the reader has to work harder to grasp the full meaning.

Oxford Level 20 (Dark Red+ Book Band)

Oliver Twist (Oxford Level 20)

What texts are like

- Storylines are more complex, involving sub-plots or parallel settings, and stories may not always be straightforwardly linear,
- There may be themes or underlying ideas in a text which are not superficially obvious,
- Texts may draw on unfamiliar contexts.

Frames
- 1-16 frames per double-page spread (average 14),
- Most frames contain some text. If a frame doesn't have text in, it is for a particular reason, i.e. the meaning can be better conveyed through artwork alone.

Sentences
- A deliberately wide variety of sentence lengths and structure in both caption boxes and speech bubbles to reflect the complexity of tone and structure found in novels at this level,
- Speech or narrative often continues across more than one caption box/speech bubble or frame including splitting a sentence between bubbles/boxes where this is effective. Connected caption boxes may be interrupted by speech bubbles and sometimes there may be more than one frame's gap between the first connected box and the second.

Language
- Challenging vocabulary is welcomed and expected,
- Classics: feature key words and phrases in the language of the original as much as possible,
- Character fiction: feature speech-like language appropriate to the characters; characters from different times and cultures may use a variety of speech styles; caption boxes give an opportunity for some more varied/literary/descriptive language as found in novels at this level,
- Non-fiction: speech bubble and caption text use widely varied language, to convey a character's speech and using technical language (which may not always be defined in context) appropriate to the topic of the book.

Inference
- Books can be structured in a less linear way, and more thought and inference is often required from the reader, to understand what is happening. The text and artwork may play more tricks on the reader now, e.g. sometimes withholding information or setting up temporary false expectations, so the reader has to work harder to grasp the full meaning.

6. Celebrating reading

In outstanding reading schools, books and reading are celebrated every day, not just on special occasions. If staff can get children excited about reading and create a buzz about books, teaching children to read becomes a much easier and more enjoyable task.

Project X *Origins* provides many opportunites to create a buzz around reading with genuinely exciting and motivating books that children will look forward to reading. **Project X** *Origins* guided reading sessions create lots of opportunities to praise children for their reading and create excitement about exploring and engaging with books. In addition here are some **Project X** inspired ideas to celebrate reading:

1. **Project X praise**: ongoing and informal praise of children's achievement is a key part of good teaching practice and guided reading sessions are an ideal time to focus on individual children. Children should also be encouraged to praise their peers and to identify and celebrate their own success. On the following pages you will find reading and writing certificate templates, featuring the **Project X** characters. These can be used to celebrate the success of individuals or groups at any point in the year.

2. **Recommended reads**: ask children to vote for their favourite **Project X** books and create a display showcasing these titles. Ask children to write recommendations for each of the books to add to the display and encourage children to recommend other books, e.g. *If you liked this, you'll love …*

3. **Project X expert**: encourage children to be an expert for the day, talking to children from their class, another class or the whole school. Children could advertise 'drop-in' times where other children can ask questions and have **Project X** books recommended to them. You could extend this to include teachers and parents.

4. **Project X day**: agree a day when the class, year or whole school can take part in **Project X** themed fun, e.g. dress like a character, re-enact their favourite stories, read their favourite books.

Certificate for FANTASTIC reading

_____

has been awarded this certificate for

_____

WELL DONE!

Signed: Max *Cat* Ant Tiger *Birdy*

Date: _____

Certificate for FANTASTIC writing

_____

has been awarded this certificate for

_____

WELL DONE!

Signed: Max *cat* Ant Tiger *Birdy*

Date: _____

© Oxford University Press 2014. Copying permitted within purchasing school only.

Name _____ Date _____

Chasing Birdy chapter analysis

Use this grid to record the key events from the story and to help you think carefully about important points in each chapter.

Chapter and key event	Why is this event important to the story?	What do we learn about the character(s) involved?	What do you think of their actions?
1: The new girl			
2: Time shift			
3: The Tick-Tock Man			
4: The Artefacts of Time			

Grey band (Oxford Level 14) ■ Chasing Birdy

Name _____   Date _____

Willows top trumps

Think about each character and rate them out of ten in the categories shown. Then have a game of top trumps with the group!

Toad
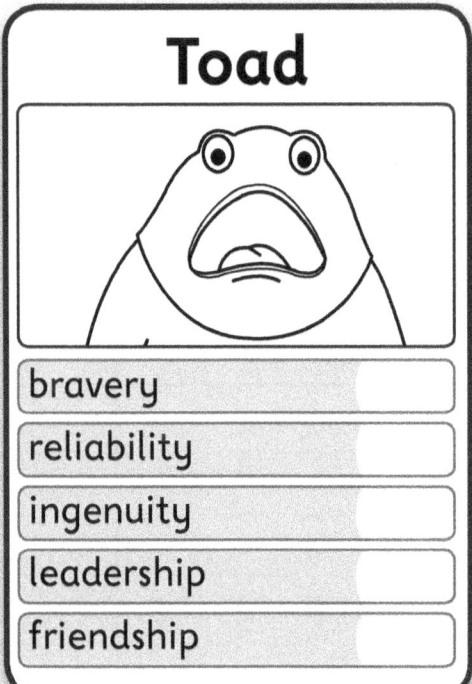
- bravery
- reliability
- ingenuity
- leadership
- friendship

Mole

- bravery
- reliability
- ingenuity
- leadership
- friendship

Badger
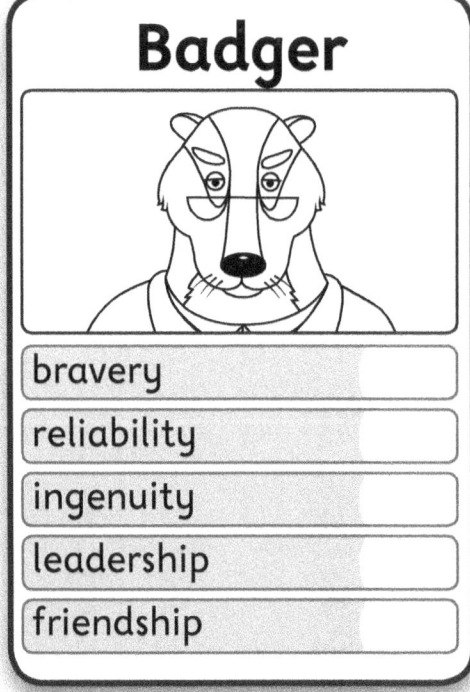
- bravery
- reliability
- ingenuity
- leadership
- friendship

Ratty
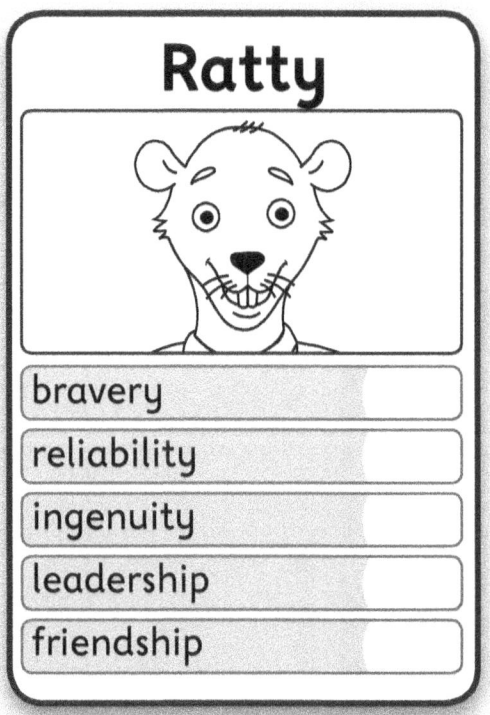
- bravery
- reliability
- ingenuity
- leadership
- friendship

Compare your scores with those of other children in your class and explain why you gave that rating, using evidence from the story.

Grey band (Oxford Level 14) ■ *The Wind in the Willows*
© Oxford University Press 2016. Copying permitted within purchasing school only.

Name _____   Date _____

Nonsense checklist

Reread each of the nonsense poems. Analyse them for nonsense features and provide evidence for each feature you find.

	Speaking animals	Objects coming to life	Rhythm, rhyme and alliteration	Made-up words	Exclamations	Unreliable narrator	Other
The Pelican Chorus							
There was an Old Man …							
The Duel							
Mr Toad							
My Shadow							

Grey band (Oxford Level 14) ■ *The Pelican Chorus and other poems*
© Oxford University Press 2016. Copying permitted within purchasing school only.

Name _____ Date _____

Great artist fact file

Create a fact file for the artist you have chosen as the greatest.

I have chosen _____ as the greatest artist of all time.

Place of birth: _____

Lived from: _____ to: _____

Early influences: _____
_____

What they were like: _____
_____

What was distinctive about their style: _____
_____
_____

Most famous work: _____
_____

Impact and influence on the world of art:
_____
_____
_____
_____
_____
_____

A portrait of my artist

Grey band (Oxford Level 14) ■ Great Artists
© Oxford University Press 2016. Copying permitted within purchasing school only.

Name _____ Date _____

About Birdy

What do we learn about Birdy from *Time Stealer*? Collect your evidence below:

Adjectives and adverbs in the text to describe her:	What she says (and how she says it):

What she does:	What others say about her:

Dark Blue band (Oxford Level 15) ■ *Time Stealer*
© Oxford University Press 2016. Copying permitted within purchasing school only.

Name _____ Date _____

Where does Mowgli belong?

Should Mowgli live with the humans or the wolf pack? Use the table below to plan your argument.

Opening statement:	
Mowgli should live with	
Points in favour	**Points against**
Conclusion:	

Useful vocabulary		
However, Firstly, Consequently, Perhaps	Surely you agree? Supporters may say On the one hand In addition,	Furthermore, It is likely To conclude,

Dark Blue band (Oxford Level 15) ■ **The Jungle Book**

Name _____ Date _____

Building vocabulary

Collect as many new or unfamiliar words or phrases as you can as you read. You can then work out the meanings as a group.

Number of new words you've learnt:

10 = Good

15 = Very good

20 = Amazing

Name _____ Date _____

'If' key messages

What are the key messages from 'If'? Write down what you think the lines on the left mean.

We think it means …				
In the poem it says …	If you can trust yourself when all men doubt you, But make allowance for their doubting too;	If you can dream—and not make dreams your master;	If you can bear to hear the truth you've spoken Twisted by knaves to make a trap for fools,	If you can force your heart and nerve and sinew To serve your turn long after they are gone,

Dark Blue band (Oxford Level 15) ■ *If and other poems*

Name _____ Date _____

Roots of invention

Use a dictionary to help you find the definitions of these words with Greek roots. Could you use any of them in your writing?

Word	Definition
epidemic	
metaphor	
democracy	
phenomenon	
symphonic	
hydraulic	
periscope	
telepathy	

Name _____   Date _____

Inventors information

Find and record key information about the different inventors in the book in the same way as the completed example.

Inventor	Key information
Archimedes	- Lived in Ancient Greece - Invented the Archimedes screw and several war weapons - Famous for working out how to measure the volume of an irregular shape (and for shouting 'Eureka!')
Johannes Gutenberg	
Thomas Edison	
Alexander Graham Bell	
Garrett Morgan	

Name _____ Date _____

Overcoming obstacles

The friends encountered a series of problems on their mission to find the sundial. Find three examples from the text and explain how the friends worked together to overcome each obstacle.

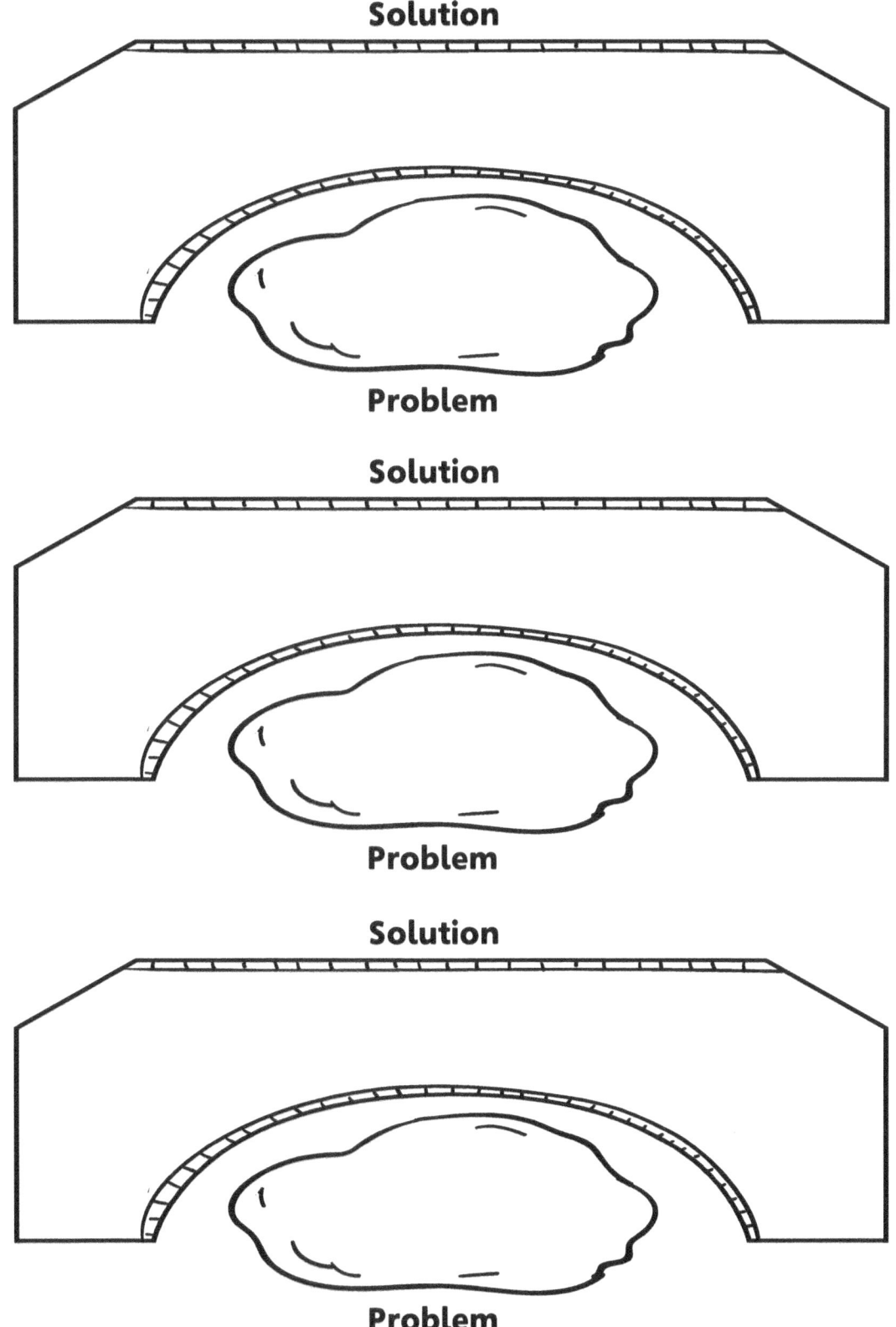

Dark Blue band (Oxford Level 16) ■ **The Sands of Deception**
© Oxford University Press 2016. Copying permitted within purchasing school only.

Name _____   Date _____

Changes in Mary

Use the chart to record how Mary changes throughout *The Secret Garden*. Collect evidence from the text to support your notes.

Chapter	What Mary is like/ how she changes	Evidence from the text
1: Misselthwaite Manor		
2: A way in		
3: In the garden		
4: Colin		
5: Homecoming		

Dark Blue band (Oxford Level 16) ■ **The Secret Garden**

Name _____ Date _____

Past, Present, Future

Think about your own feelings towards the past, the present and the future and try to describe each with a metaphor drawn from nature. (Hint: it might be helpful to look at photographs of nature.)

"What the past is like to thee?"

"Tell me, what is the present hour?"

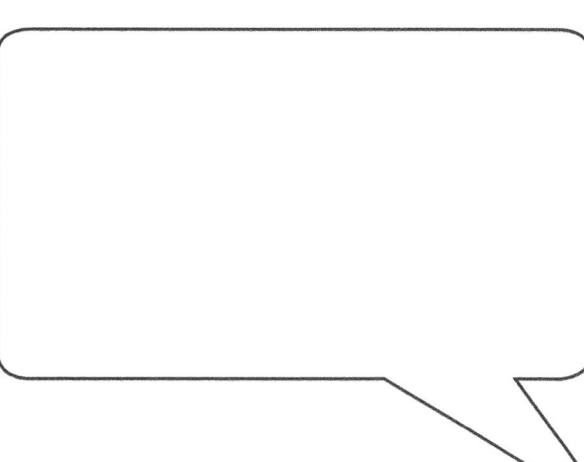

"And what is the future, happy one?"

Dark Blue band (Oxford Level 16) ■ *I Wandered Lonely as a Cloud and other poems*
© Oxford University Press 2016. Copying permitted within purchasing school only.

Name _____ Date _____

Nobel Prize

Choose two naturalists from the text and take notes to show their main observations, including key locations and dates, inside the magnifying glasses.

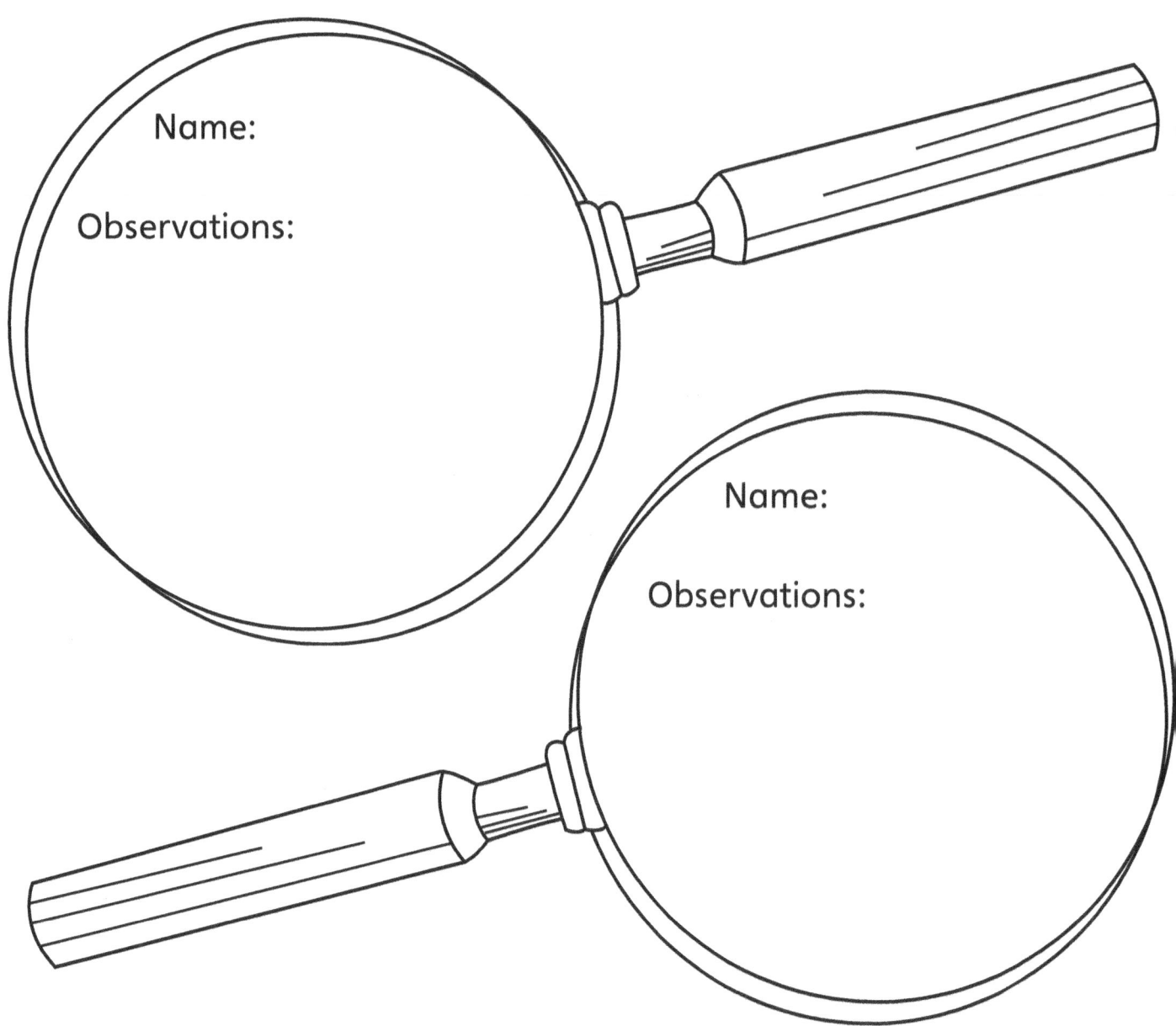

Which naturalist would you award the Nobel prize to and why?

_____

_____

Dark Blue band (Oxford Level 16) ■ Great Naturalists
© Oxford University Press 2016. Copying permitted within purchasing school only.

Terrific talk

Turn these speech bubbles into descriptive text, using adverbs or powerful synonyms to show how they are said.

> We can't let a little thing like AN ARMY stop us!

_____
_____
_____
_____

> It is amazing up close, isn't it?

_____
_____
_____
_____

> Birdy … Birdy?

_____
_____
_____
_____

> We have to do something!

_____
_____
_____
_____

Dark Red band (Oxford Level 17) ■ **The Jurchen Recruits**

Name _____   Date _____

Jeopardy!

Identify the points where the friends face danger in *The Jurchen Recruits*. How do they escape?

Danger ...	How they escape ...
The team drop the Escape Wheel.	They link arms and spin round so they can reach it.

Dark Red band (Oxford Level 17) ■ The Jurchen Recruits

Name _____ Date _____

Studying Long John Silver

Use the chart to record what we learn about Long John Silver as the story progresses. Collect evidence from the text to support your notes.

Chapter	What do we know?	Evidence from the text
1: The map		
2: The mutiny		
3: Jim's adventure		
4: Captain Flint's treasure		

Name _____ Date _____

Pied Piper glossary

Create a glossary for *The Pied Piper of Hamelin* below. Use a dictionary or the Internet to help you with the definitions.

Word	Definition

Name _____ Date _____

Poetic devices

Can you find examples of the different poetic devices used in *The Pied Piper of Hamelin*?

Device	Definition	Examples
Repetition	Words or phrases being repeated	
Alliteration	Repetition of a sound	
Personification	Giving human qualities to objects or creatures	
Assonance	Repetition of soft vowel sounds	
Dynamic verbs	Verbs of action to increase the pace	
Similes	Comparisons using 'as' or 'like'	
Metaphors	Making comparisons through ideas or images	

Dark Red band (Oxford Level 17) ■ **The Pied Piper of Hamelin**
© Oxford University Press 2016. Copying permitted within purchasing school only.

Name _____ Date _____

Is it non-fiction?

How is *Great Space Explorers* like other non-fiction texts you've read? How is it different?

Similar	Different

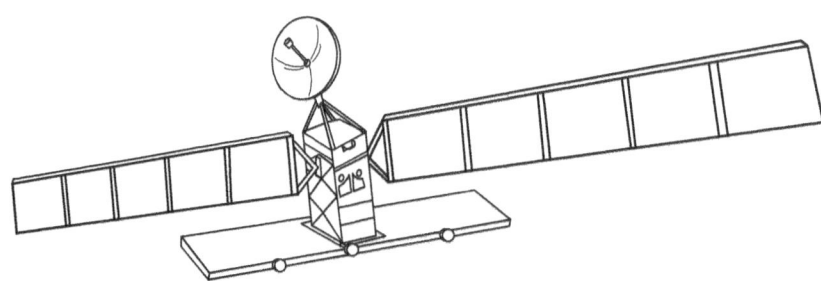

Dark Red band (Oxford Level 17) ■ **Great Space Explorers**
© Oxford University Press 2016. Copying permitted within purchasing school only.nly.

Name _____   Date _____

Great -ough words

Find words in *Great Space Explorers* that contain the same *-ough* sounds as the words in the table below. Add these words as well as your own to complete the table.

Examples	Matching *-ough* sounds
bought	
rough	
cough	
though	
borough	
plough	

Dark Red band (Oxford Level 17) — Great Space Explorers
© Oxford University Press 2016. Copying permitted within purchasing school only.

Name _____   Date _____

Leading the way

Identify the ways in which Max and Birdy demonstrate leadership. Which skills do they share? How are their leadership styles different? Use the diagram below to note down your ideas and explain your thoughts to a partner.

Dark Red band (Oxford Level 18) ■ Time's Pendulum
© Oxford University Press 2016. Copying permitted within purchasing school only.

Name _____   Date _____

About Alice

Choose four character traits that you admire most about Alice and explain what she does or says in the story to demonstrate these.

Dark Red band (Oxford Level 18) ■ Alice's Adventures in Wonderland

Name _____ Date _____

Jabberwocky

Write some suitable real words in place of the nonsense words that have been omitted from the first two verses of the poem. Remember to retain the atmosphere of the original.

'Twas _____, and the _____
Did _____ and _____ in the _____;
All _____ were the _____,
And the _____ _____ _____.

'Beware the _____, my son!
The jaws that bite, the claws that catch!
Beware the _____ bird, and shun
The _____ _____!'

Name _____ Date _____

Great scientist plaque

Choose the scientist you most admire from the text and design a plaque to commemorate their achievements. Include:

- key dates and places,
- significant discoveries,
- obstacles overcome,
- personality traits that helped them become a great scientist,
- how their work is still influencing us today.

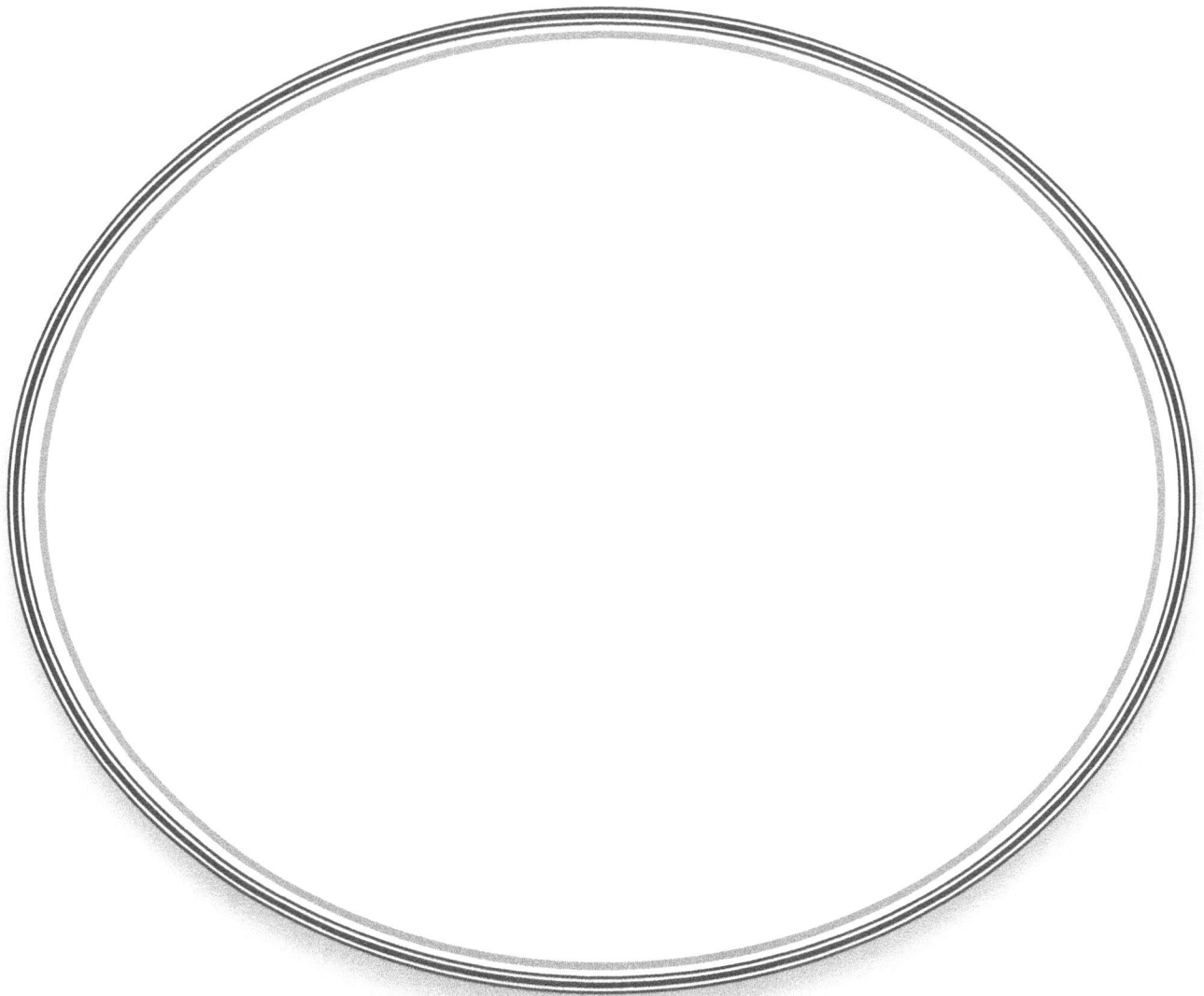

Captain Cook play-script

(Aboard the Resolution.)

Narrator:	The other ship was gliding smoothly in their direction, its prow slicing through the icy water.
First Mate:	That's impossible. It looks just like our ship.
Sailor 1:	Aye, it's a perfect copy of the *Resolution*.
First Mate:	I can't see a single soul on board.
Sailor 2 (*shouting*):	CAPTAIN!
Captain Cook (*to the children*):	How did you escape from the brig?
First Mate:	Captain, before you deal with them, there is something you have to see.
First Mate:	It's a ship, sir. The name on the side reads *Resolution*!
Narrator:	The other ship was getting ever closer.
Max (*to Birdy*):	Are you thinking what I'm thinking?
Max:	Err, Captain …
Captain Cook:	What is it?
Birdy:	It's about that ship …
Narrator:	But there was no time for Birdy to explain.
First Mate:	Captain! There's something else …
Captain Cook (*looking through his telescope*):	What's that on deck? It looks like no sailor I've ever seen!
Max:	That's because it's not a real sailor …
Captain Cook:	Not a real sailor?
Birdy:	It's not human.
First Mate:	What's the girl blabbering about?
Captain Cook:	Let her speak.
Birdy:	It's a machine.
Captain Cook:	A *machine*?
First Mate:	Captain, there are even more of them.
Birdy:	It's your sea clock they're after. We tried to tell you earlier.
Tiger:	Yeah, before you locked us up!
Captain Cook:	What do these machines want with my timepiece?
Max:	They are collecting important clocks. Your sea clock is more valuable than you realize.
Narrator:	The Tick-Tock ship no longer looked deserted, and it was closing in on the real *Resolution*. Fast!

Name _____ Date _____

Buck's life

Collect words and phrases that tell you about Buck's life from before and after he is sold.

Before	After

Dark Red+ band (Oxford Level 19) ■ **The Call of the Wild**

Name _____   Date _____

Spot the device!

Can you find examples of the different poetic devices used in the poem you are studying?

Device	Definition	Examples
Repetition	Words or phrases being repeated	
Alliteration	Repetition of a constant sound	
Assonance	Repetition of soft vowel sounds	
Internal rhyme	A rhyme within one line of the poem	
Figurative language	Using words and phrases beyond their literal sense. Includes similes and metaphors.	
Personification	Giving human qualities to objects or creatures	

Which device did you find the most powerful? Why? _____

_____

Dark Red+ band (Oxford Level 19) ■ *The Raven and other poems*
© Oxford University Press 2016. Copying permitted within purchasing school only.

Name _____ Date _____

Talking about poems

Consider the following statements. Which poems best relate to these statements?

> It uses some old-fashioned words but this makes it more interesting to read.

_____
_____
_____
_____
_____
_____

> The words the poet uses paint a perfect picture of this creature.

_____
_____
_____
_____
_____
_____

> This is a difficult poem to read, but once you understand it, it's wonderful.

_____
_____
_____
_____
_____
_____

Name _____ Date _____

Engaging engineers

How does *Great Engineers* try to share information in an engaging way? Record your ideas below.

Features	Language
− Graphic novel style drawings	− Chatty language from Brunel as he talks to the reader

Name _____ Date _____

About Kalvin Spearhead

Can you find evidence from the text about Kalvin Spearhead's character and why he behaves as he does?

| Description in the text: | His words: |
|---|---|ованной

| His actions: | His past: |

Dark Red+ band (Oxford Level 20) ■ Time Runs Out
© Oxford University Press 2016. Copying permitted within purchasing school only.

Name _____ Date _____

About Mr Bumble

What does the text tell you about Mr Bumble? Collect your evidence below.

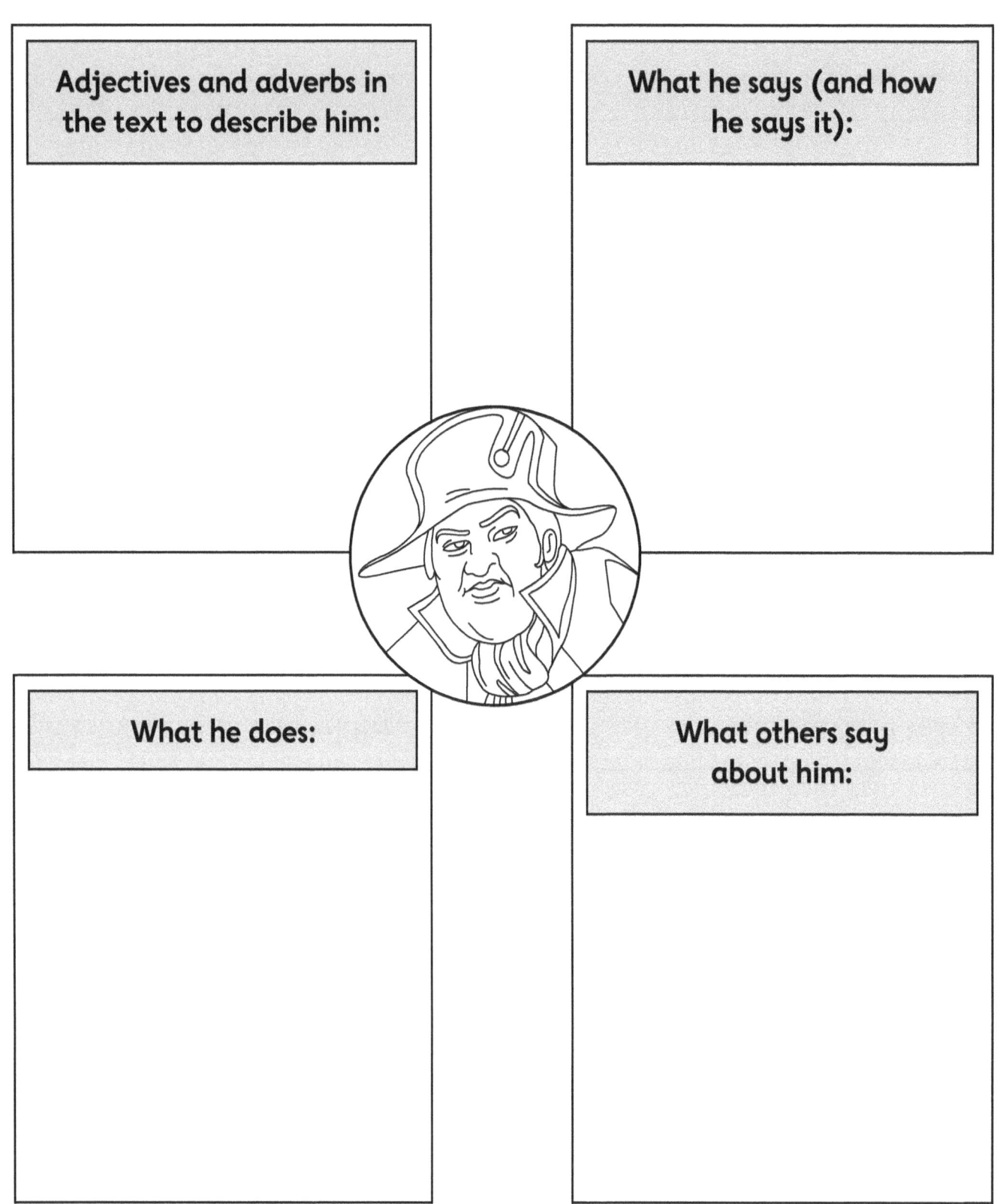

Adjectives and adverbs in the text to describe him:

What he says (and how he says it):

What he does:

What others say about him:

Dark Red+ band (Oxford Level 20) ■ Oliver Twist

Name _____   Date _____

What it means to me

Find examples of each poetic device in the text and then use these examples to explain what you think this poem is about.

Poem: _____

Poetic device	Examples
Repetition	
Figurative language	
Personification	
Use of adjectives	
Powerful verbs	
Poetic images	

I think this poem is about _____

_____

Dark Red+ band (Oxford Level 20) ■ For the Fallen and other poems
© Oxford University Press 2016. Copying permitted within purchasing school only.

Name _____ Date _____

Greatest pioneer

Use the table below to plan your argument for who is the greatest pioneer.

Our pioneer is:	
Achievements:	Personal qualities:
Challenges:	Impact on the world:

Useful Vocabulary		
However, Firstly, Consequently, Perhaps	Some people believe Surely you agree? Supporters may say On the one hand	In addition, Furthermore, It is likely To conclude,

Dark Red+ band (Oxford Level 20) — Great Pioneers

Great Pioneers first draft

Can you improve this first draft of *Great Pioneers*? Rewrite the passage below, correcting any typing errors and mistakes.

> Pioneers are Trail Blazers: people who lead the way in what they do. A pioneer could be the first person to visit some where that know ones ever been before. a pioneer might make something that changes the world. A pioneer can be someone what discovers something knew. Pioneers, of science could work for years to solve a problem that effects our daily lives.
>
> You need determination. You need to be inventive and tenatious. So you keep going when things go wrong. Sometimes you also need a bit of luck.

Name _____ Date _____

Balanced argument

Use the table below to plan a balanced argument.

Opening statement:	
Points in favour	**Points against**
Conclusion:	

Useful vocabulary		
However,	Some people believe	In addition,
Firstly,	Surely you agree?	Furthermore,
Consequently,	Supporters may say	It is likely
Perhaps	On the one hand	To conclude,

Name _____ Date _____

Performance evaluation

Make notes on each performance, including positives and things to improve.

Name:	Positives:	To improve next time:

© Oxford University Press 2016. Copying permitted within purchasing school only.

Name _____ Date _____

Story planning frame

Make brief notes or draw quick sketches of what is going to happen in your story.

Main characters	Setting or settings

What happens at the beginning?

What problem or complication occurs?

How is this resolved?

How does the story end?

Name _____ Date _____

KWL

Fill in the grid to show what you know, what you would like to know and what you have learnt.

Next steps *(new questions, new enquiries)*	
What I have learnt	
What I would like to find out	
What I already know	

Name _____ Date _____

Vocabulary bookmark

Cut out the bookmarks and stick to pieces of card.

This belongs to

_____

List at least three new or unusual words you find as you read

_____ page ____

_____ page ____

_____ page ____

_____ page ____

_____ page ____

_____ page ____

This belongs to

_____

List at least three new or unusual words you find as you read

_____ page ____

_____ page ____

_____ page ____

_____ page ____

_____ page ____

_____ page ____

© Oxford University Press 2016. Copying permitted within purchasing school only.

Name _____ Date _____

Spelling sort

Label each sort box with its spelling pattern *(e.g. ible/able or tion/sion)*. Add examples of words spelt in this way to the boxes.

- - - - - - - - - - - - - -	- - - - - - - - - - - - - -	- - - - - - - - - - - - - -

Dictated sentences

Ask a partner to make up an oral sentence containing one or more of the words. Can you write the sentence?

1. _____

_____

2. _____

_____

3. _____

_____

Name _____   Date _____

Discussion prompt bookmark

Cut out the bookmarks. Use them when reading to remind you of ideas you can discuss with your group.

Why did …?

What if …?

I didn't understand …

I can picture …

I loved the part when …

I had a question about …

Why did …?

What if …?

I didn't understand …

I can picture …

I loved the part when …

I had a question about …

Name _____ Date _____

Synthesizing grid

Use this chart to help you make links between information and clues in different parts of a book. What new information can you work out by combining ideas from different parts of the book?

Book title Author		
I found this out on page …	I found this out on page …	These two things together tell me …
I found this out on page …	I found this out on page …	These two things together tell me …
I found this out on page …	I found this out on page …	These two things together tell me …

Name _____ Date _____

Prediction and reflection grid

What do you predict might happen?
Make notes in the first two columns before you read.
After you have read, make notes in the third column on what did happen. Compare what you have written in the first and third columns.

Book title Author		
I think this might happen …	**I think this because …**	**What did happen**

Project Origins

© Oxford University Press 2016. Copying permitted within purchasing school only.